CHARLOTTE
MOTOR SPEEDWAY

Greg Fielden

MBI Publishing Company

First published in 2000 by MBI Publishing Company, 729 Prospect Avenue, PO Box 1, Osceola, WI 54020-0001 USA

MBI Publishing Company books are also available at discounts in bulk quantity for industrial or sales-promotional use. For details write to Special Sales Manager at Motorbooks International Wholesalers & Distributors, 729 Prospect Avenue, PO Box 1, Osceola, WI 54020-0001 USA.

Library of Congress Cataloging-in-Publication Data
Fielden, Greg.
 Charlotte Motor Speedway / Greg Fielden.
   p.cm.
 Includes index.
 ISBN 0-7603-0751-2 (pbk. : alk. paper)
   1. Charlotte Motor Speedway (Organization)—History. 2. Stock car racing—North Carolina—Charlotte—History. I. Title.

GV1033.5.C53 F54 2000
796.72'06'875676--dc21

On the front cover: Jimmy Pardue's No. 54 Burton-Robinson Plymouth is shown leading the 1964 World 600 with Paul Goldsmith (No. 25) and Bobby Isaac (No. 26) in tow. Eventually all three drivers dropped out of the race with engine problems. Jim Paschal guided a Petty Enterprises Plymouth to a victory by a four-lap margin over teammate Richard Petty.

Frontis: Two days before the 1986 Coca-Cola 600, Richard Petty crashed his Pontiac during a practice run. NASCAR did not permit Petty to enter a back-up car. Privateer D. K. Ulrich offered to let Petty start his No. 6 Chevrolet in the 600. Petty accepted, and it was the last time King Richard drove in NASCAR Winston Cup competition in any car number other than 43. *CMS Archives*

Title page: The 24,000-plus horsepower of the 1976 National 500's starting grid thunders through the first turn at Charlotte Motor Speedway with David Pearson and Buddy Baker leading the way. Neither driver would take the win on this day. Instead, Donnie Allison took his Hoss Ellington Chevrolet to victory circle. *CMS Archives*

Back cover top: Roush Racing's Jeff Burton hit one of the biggest paydays of his career by taking his Ford to victory over Bobby Labonte's Pontiac in the 1999 Coca-Cola 600. *Tom Riles*

Back cover bottom: The wonder boy of modern NASCAR racing, Jeff Gordon, took his Chevy Monte Carlo to Victory Lane in the 1997 Coca-Cola 600 held at Charlotte Motor Speedway. Jeff Gordon became a force to be reckoned with virtually overnight. From 1994 to 1998, Gordon won five consecutive poles for the annual May running of the Coca-Cola 500, and recorded victories in NASCAR Winston Cup racing's most demanding event in 1994, 1997, and 1998. *CMS photo by Chuck Burton*

Edited by Paul Johnson
Designed by Dan Perry

Printed in China

CONTENTS

FOREWORD
By Buddy Baker

When I first stepped onto the grounds of Charlotte Motor Speedway in the spring of 1960, it looked like the surface of the moon. There wasn't a blade of grass anywhere, there was a deep crater in the infield between the third and fourth turns, and there was a huge mountain of rock on the other end of the infield.

The only thing that looked remotely familiar to me was the one-and-a-half-mile circular strip of asphalt surrounding this patch of unearthliness. And it wasn't long before the pavement came apart. It, too, developed large holes and craters during the opening practice session. The whole place looked like something out of *The Twilight Zone.* I think Rod Serling might have even been standing on pit lane during one of my many pit stops in the first race.

I was driving a car owned by Ankrum "Spook" Crawford in the first World 600 on June 19, 1960. Most of the cars in the race were equipped with protective chicken wire and windshield screens to guard against flying asphalt. That first race was clearly a survival of the fittest contest; I was one of the few to "survive" the entire 600 miles. I finished 19th in the field of 60. I remember we all started three abreast that day. I started on the outside of the 16th row.

The race lasted nearly six hours and Joe Lee Johnson's average winning speed wasn't much over 100 miles per hour. Six drivers, including Lee and Richard Petty and Junior Johnson, were disqualified for cutting across the dusty infield area between the front chute and the pits, which kicked up clouds of dust that lingered in the air and obscured vision. The attendance that day was somewhere around 30,000. The spectators could have used mountain climbing gear to scale the steep embankment leading to the grandstands.

Today, Charlotte's Lowe's Motor Speedway is clearly the Taj Mahal of motorsports, attracting crowds of nearly 200,000 for its spectacular events. The track surface is billiard-table smooth, the craters and mountains are long gone, elevators take spectators to the plush suites high atop the grandstands, and the entire facility is a first-class representation of our sport of stock car racing.

During my career as a NASCAR Winston Cup driver, I was fortunate enough to win four races at Charlotte. My first career win came in the 1967 National 500, driving a Dodge for master mechanic and team owner Ray Fox. I happened to be the one who broke Richard Petty's record-setting 10-race winning streak, but I never thought of that. In fact, I did not realize that I had snapped his streak until someone pointed it out to me. For me the victory meant my career had been fulfilled, and the frog had finally received a kiss. Ray Fox was the first top team owner to give me a chance in factory-backed equipment, and I wanted so badly to win for him. Like the Speedway, my career had a rocky start, but when I won at Charlotte Motor Speedway for the first time, I felt like I had made the grade as a race car driver.

I won at Charlotte again in 1968 with Fox, and got victories with Petty Enterprises in 1972 and Harry Hyde and Nord Krauskopf's team in 1973. And I can honestly say that all four of those wins on my hometown track are among my most cherished memories.

That's one of the few things that has never changed about Charlotte's Lowe's Motor Speedway. All of the drivers want a victory at Charlotte on their résumé. The Winston Cup races and the All-Star event are three of the most important races on the annual NASCAR calendar. Winning a single race at Charlotte can make a driver's career.

With its managerial leadership, Charlotte's Lowe's Motor Speedway has become one of the entertainment capitals of the country. No matter the size of the stadium, you still have to put on a good show, which is always the case at Charlotte. From the entertaining pre-race show to the energized qualifying under the lights and the excitement of the 500- and 600-mile races, everything has become a special event at Charlotte's Lowe's Motor Speedway.

ACKNOWLEDGMENTS

Numerous individuals have combined their efforts to make the production of this book possible. From the management of Charlotte's Lowe's Motor Speedway to the dozens of photographers whose work graces these pages, the author extends his profound admiration and gratitude.

The author offers gratitude to Bruton Smith, Humpy Wheeler, and the entire staff of Charlotte's Lowe's Motor Speedway, and a special tip of the hat to Publicity Director Jerry Gappens and his fine supporting cast. Brad Bowling, Director of Web Site Development, has been one of the most influential forces behind this effort. Thanks, Brad, for your tireless efforts.

Nearly all of the images that appear on these pages came from the vast photo files at Charlotte's Lowe's Motor Speedway. Many thanks to Photo Director Harold Hinson for permitting the author to roam through the vast expanse of photo files. Without Hinson's courteous and generous support, the completion of this project would not have been possible. And a special thanks is extended to Deneen Goforth, Office Administrator at Charlotte's Lowe's Motor Speedway, who always delivered a cheerful smile and professional logistical support.

Many of the nostalgic images were snapped by T. Taylor Warren and Don Hunter, two photographers who have been capturing images at hundreds of speedways across the country for nearly a half century. Both Warren and Hunter were trackside during NASCAR's formative years and their contributions to auto racing have been invaluable. Without these two individuals and their meticulous work, NASCAR Grand National and Winston Cup racing would not have been documented as well as it has.

Dozens of the black-and-white photos and color transparencies included herein had no photo credit listed. For this study, these images have been credited as Charlotte Motor Speedway (CMS) Archives. Some of the accredited photographers include Pal Parker and Bryant McMurray, both of whom headed the Photo Department and snapped the shutter thousands of times over the years on behalf of the Speedway. Thanks also to Graham Niven, David Chobat, and Brian Czobat, three photographers for whom the author has the highest regard and whose photographs are signatures in themselves. And to Bryan Hallman, who stepped in at the eleventh hour to supply badly needed images. It is indeed an honor and a privilege to have Hallman's quality work included within these pages.

Other photographers whose efforts appear in these pages include David Allio, Bill Niven, Chuck Burton, Lin Webb, Jeffrey S. Johnson, H. J. Rudes, G. B. Warren, E. Lee Roane, Terry Renna, Mike Hamilton, and Tom Riles. Undoubtedly there are others who have contributed as well.

Additional thanks are extended to Pat Fielden, Dorothy Davis, and Ruth and Cindy Garbarini, who generously assisted in proofing, software components, and inspiration to conclude this project.

And last, but certainly not least, a special gratitude goes to the participants in the sport of NASCAR Winston Cup stock car racing. To the drivers, owners, promoters, crew members, sponsors, manufacturers, and many others who form this close-knit fraternity, a heartfelt special thanks for making the sport what it once was and guiding it to what it has become. The participants of this sport are the people who have written this book. All the author has done is put it between two covers.

INTRODUCTION

The little Dutch boy who saved his town by putting his finger in a hole in the dike had a simple assignment compared to the task of building Charlotte's Lowe's Motor Speedway. This was not a prosaic, ordinary, run-of-the-mill task. Seemingly insurmountable obstacles had to be cleared before and after the first spade of dirt was turned.

Forty-one years ago two men, Curtis Turner and Bruton Smith, fostered ideas of building a grandiose speedway on the outskirts of North Carolina's Queen City. NASCAR's premier stock car racing series once traveled on ramshackle roads between Southern hamlets, racing in tumbletown stadia before handfuls of people. Turner and Smith had visions of a first-class facility, one that would draw thousands of spectators. Combining their tireless efforts with meager resources, they embarked on a daring adventure.

The adventure proved a rough and rocky road. When the track opened in June 1960, it had a disheveled appearance. The track was in a state of disorder, a veritable minefield during the entire grand opening. The race became a survival of the fittest.

The inaugural race was neither an artistic nor a financial success. Revenues did not come close to satisfying creditors. In less than two years, Charlotte Motor Speedway fell into the shackles and chains of bankruptcy. The fact that it was able to survive at all smacks of miracles. That it thrives today is truly amazing, considering its start.

Its path to solvency is remarkable. Its projected path for the future is mind-boggling. By any yardstick, Charlotte Motor Speedway is one of the most lavish facilities in motorsports. It may have the most plush VIP suites of any sporting facility in the country.

A special attitude and polished skills were required to produce the lofty status the Speedway enjoys today. Since his return to power at the Speedway in the mid-1970s, Bruton Smith has provided the impetus that has carried the sport over into the era of organization and massive expansion. In order to keep up with the demands of a burgeoning sport bursting at the seams, Charlotte's Lowe's Motor Speedway has set the pace in providing first-class facilities for the participants and the spectators.

As we approach the new millennium, Charlotte's Lowe's Motor Speedway is the second-largest motorsports stadium in the country, with 167,254 permanent seats. Another elaborate tower grandstand structure will be completed by May 2000.

"The additional seating makes us second only to Indianapolis Motor Speedway in overall capacity," said President and General Manager Humpy Wheeler, who has a deep and abiding affection for homegrown American sports. "With all the racetracks around the country being improved or built from scratch, our challenge is to keep our speedway the premier facility in all of motorsports. To do this we must continue to be innovative and timely with new additions such as the $14 million Ford Grandstand. The structure includes unique amenities for additional Speedway Club memberships, corporate sales as well as the avid race fan."

The main attractions at the speedway are the NASCAR Winston Cup and Busch Series events. The Coca-Cola 600, staged annually in May, is regarded as the second-most important event on the annual NASCAR Winston Cup schedule behind the Daytona 500. Since 1960, the longest and most-grueling stock car race has demanded feats of stamina that strain comprehension. It has produced splendid success stories as well as breathtaking heartbreak. The spectacle, framed by green and checkered flags, has been irresistibly appealing for 40 years.

The enormous crowds who annually flock to Charlotte's Lowe's Motor Speedway are lured by the excitement, color, noise, and revelry that major league stock car racing has to offer. The explosion of interest in NASCAR Winston Cup racing crosses social, economic, and intellectual lines. From its major league stock car offerings to the support events, the custom auto fairs, various charitable functions, and swanky upscale happenings, Charlotte's Lowe's Motor Speedway provides quality attractions in a comfortable atmosphere.

In 1960, Bruton Smith said, "It is with everyone in mind that we at Charlotte Motor Speedway strive to provide the best entertainment possible. Without respect to any particular order, we are thinking of the drivers, the fans, the car owners, the manufacturers, the mechanics, the officials, and everyone else. The slogan we have followed from the very beginning has been 'Charlotte Motor Speedway, it's for everyone,' and it will be with this in mind that we will continue to work." Forty years later, that statement still applies.

The genesis and development of Charlotte's Lowe's Motor Speedway have been told and retold as part of NASCAR's cultural legacy. This book focuses on the role the speedway has had in the evolution of America's fastest-growing sport. It will spotlight the high-octane machines that have graced the high-banked mile-and-a-half speedway for four decades, and the supremely gifted drivers whose quick reflexes are put to amazing tests. It will also trace the lineage of the track itself, which has become one of America's most endearing and unlikely success stories.

CHAPTER 1

Mission Impossible

CONSTRUCTION OF THE CHARLOTTE MOTOR SPEEDWAY

T he National Association of Stock Car Auto Racing (NASCAR) was incorporated in February of 1948 in Daytona Beach, Florida, following a series of meetings among the South's most influential motorsports figures. Together they laid the groundwork and mapped plans for a national sanctioning body to tie the loose threads and govern the sport of stock car racing, which had been little more than a wildcat adventure for a gang of rambunctious roughnecks. Under the guidance of NASCAR President Bill France, Sr., the landscape of stock car racing gained a measure of organization, and the frenzied freedom of motorized competition stretched out to hundreds of hamlets throughout rural America.

Delays in construction forced the three-week postponement of the first World 600 at Charlotte Motor Speedway. The original race date was May 29, 1960, but the race was actually run on June 19, 1960. One of the first structures built on the 550-acre tract of land adjacent to a lightly traveled U.S. Highway 29 was the huge white sign advertising the inaugural event. The posted awards of $100,000 were the first NASCAR event with a six-digit payoff. *CMS photo by G. B. Warren*

The first on-site ticket office for Charlotte Motor Speedway was an antique white two-level house. Built in 1774, it was the home of North Carolina's first elected governor, Nathaniel Alexander. According to legend, George Washington was said to have visited the house in 1805 during his tour of the nation. While a graveyard, smoke house, and other rickety structures were razed during construction, this house, with its white, weathered boards covering the original walls of hand-hewn logs, remained. It was eventually leveled in the late 1970s.
CMS photo by T. Taylor Warren

In the formative years, NASCAR championship stock car racing events were presented on a wide variety of rough, dusty, dirt tracks, most of which were surrounded by scraggly fences of undressed lumber. The track surfaces, for the most part, had the texture of a washboard. Spectator comforts were confined to a splintered piece of wood in a swaying structure loosely defined as a grandstand. But despite the rustic beginnings, NASCAR's newfangled brand of auto racing flourished throughout the South.

By the late 1950s, the theater of stock car racing was expanding. The sprawling new Daytona International Speedway, which opened in February of 1959, delivered a cachet of sorts for the entire sport, and the new and fancier playgrounds were needed to keep the momentum advancing forward.

Shortly after the conclusion of the inaugural Speedweek activities at Daytona, renowned racer Curtis Turner told a small group of business associates that he intended to build a superspeedway near Charlotte,

North Carolina. Turner had been part of the fabric of NASCAR racing since its dawn, and the big Virginian established himself as a champion driver of unrivaled skill as well as a businessman of considerable merit in the timber industry.

Coincidentally, Olin Bruton Smith, short-track promoter par excellence, had been toying with the idea of constructing a huge speedway with all the trimmings—and the Charlotte area was his target as well. Smith, often regarded as the most prescient short-track promoter in the Carolinas, had as early as 1955 been nursing ideas that Charlotte was the ideal location for an all-purpose facility.

Turner declared that his Charlotte Motor Speedway would be built despite the fact that no financing whatsoever had been secured for the enormous project. Addressing his small group of colleagues, Turner held up the keys to his Apache airplane and a Diners Club credit card and asserted, "These, plus faith, energy, and work will get the job done, for as we say in the timber

The first officers and board of directors of Charlotte Motor Speedway were all prominent businessmen in the Southeast. Pictured left to right are: A. C. Goines of Charlotte, secretary and treasurer of the America Mortgage and Investment Corporation of Charlotte, who would serve as president of the speedway in 1963; G. D. Smith of Big Island, Virginia, an executive of the Bank of Big Island; Bruton Smith of Oakboro, North Carolina, a veteran short-track promoter and executive vice president and general manager of Charlotte Motor Speedway; Curtis Turner of Roanoke, Virginia, president of the new speedway and Turner Timber Corporation, which had its main offices in Charlotte; Jerry Ball of Charlotte, a retired public relations director of Esso Standard Oil Company and a popular musical entertainer; and G. B. Nalley of Easley, South Carolina, a timberman, financier, and real estate executive. Not pictured is Charles Crutchfield of Charlotte, vice president and general manger of Jefferson Standard Broadcasting Company. *CMS Archives*

The noble task of constructing Charlotte Motor Speedway began in July of 1959. The site of the huge plant was an alternate selection located by Richard Phillips, who was a partner with Curtis Turner in the timber industry, after the prime Arrowood Industrial location along U.S. Highway 49 became unobtainable. In the beginning, it seemed virtually impossible for a two- to three-year project to be completed in 11 months. *CMS Archives*

During the early stages of construction, track president Curtis Turner would often drive his Cadillac onto the site, unable to resist kicking up a little dust as he whipped his luxury vehicle along what would eventually become the Speedway's front stretch. *CMS photo by Don Hunter*

business, 'The difficult we do immediately; the impossible takes a little longer.' "

Both auto racing icons made public announcements about their grand projects in April of 1959. After exploring several different locations, Turner settled on a 550-acre tract of land bordering U.S. Highway 29 north of Charlotte, just inside the Cabarrus County line. Smith's original plans for his Charlotte International Speedway were on a location south of Charlotte in Pineville, near the site of a gigantic board track that had been built in 1924. The 1.25-mile oval with towering 40-degree banking in the turns was the scene of open wheel racing for four years before the wooden track succumbed to termites, weather, and other harsh elements.

The consensus was that two tracks in the Charlotte area would reduce the chances of survival for either. Turner and Smith eventually merged and pooled their efforts. Wise heads prevailed over hard ones, and discretion became the better part of valor. Turner, an outgoing eccentric of extraordinary fortitude, became president of Charlotte Motor Speedway. Smith, the consummate promoter keenly aware of the complex,

The narrow two-lane tunnel located in the fourth turn was the only access to the Speedway infield other than the usual cross-over gates. The tunnel was not particularly wide or tall, but there were no team transporters or campers utilized by spectators in 1960. *CMS Archives*

Charlotte's First Big Track

Charlotte's first venture into the world of big-league auto racing came in the 1920s. A 1.25-mile oval constructed entirely of green pinewood laid edgewise provided electrifying speeds, an economic boon for the Queen City, and a series of spine-tingling races that now lie in the dusty recesses of auto racing's history pages.

Four million feet of prime Carolina lumber and 80 tons of nails and spikes went into the construction of Charlotte Speedway, which staged its first race on October 25, 1924. From the time the track was conceived by a group of businessmen to the time the huge plant was completed was a shade over one month! An army of 300 workers, mostly carpenters, labored in 18-hour shifts for 40 days to complete the project. Cost of construction was pegged at $380,000, a tidy sum in 1924.

The two straightaways were only 792 feet in length, tied together by wide, sweeping turns, each measuring 2,508 feet. The turns were built on towering stilts, angled upward at 40 degrees, 7 degrees steeper than Talladega Superspeedway. Wooden grandstands were placed on both straightaways. At its completion, Charlotte Speedway was labeled the most beautiful and modern speedway in America.

Located on a 283-acre site on Route 26 in Pineville, 10 miles south of Charlotte and adjacent to the railroad, Charlotte Speedway was easily accessible. Virtually all of the big speedways of that era were constructed near train stations and the racing machinery was transported to the track by rail.

The magnificent speedway opened with a tragic footnote. Nine days before the first event, Ernie Ansterberg, a member of the powerful Duesenberg Racing Team, was killed during the track's initial practice session. It would prove to be the only fatality in the Speedway's brief history.

Twelve thoroughbred open-wheel race cars started the first 200-lap, 250-mile championship event. A crowd of close to 50,000 was on hand to witness the historic event. Peter DePaolo, who would win the Indianapolis 500 the following May, topped the qualifying charts with a speed of 132.8 miles per hour. Two-time national driving champion Earl Cooper was flagged the winner of the inaugural event, but following a check of the scoring tape, Tommy Milton was officially declared the victor at an average speed of 118.171 miles per hour. He drove a finely tuned Miller Special equipped with a 122-ci engine!

Cooper came back to win the second 250-miler held on May 11, 1925, and Milton won again in the November 11, 1925, race. Four weekends of activity highlighted the schedule in 1926 with the format changed in mid-season. Long-distance marathons were replaced by a series of heat races and intermediate-distance feature events.

A pair of championship events was staged in 1927 with Peter DePaolo and Babe Stapp sharing Victory Circle. Frank Lockhart established a new one-lap track record of 132.890 miles per hour in qualifications.

By late 1927, the condition of Charlotte Speedway was deteriorating. Board tracks of the teens and twenties were susceptible to a wide variety of elements. Harsh winters, scalding summers, annual rainfall, and termites took their toll on the pines, and they would often work loose, splinter, and decay beyond repair. Charlotte Speedway was a victim of these elements and never reopened after the 1927 season.

A smooth ribbon of pavement was laid in April and May of 1960. At this point, there were no infield structures or garage stalls in place, pit road was nonexistent, and work on the concrete grandstand had only just begun. *CMS Archives*

When construction of the Speedway fell behind schedule, light poles were erected along the homestretch so construction crews could work around the clock. This photo was taken in mid-May of 1960, scarcely a month before practice sessions began in preparation for the inaugural World 600. *CMS Archives*

shifting panorama of stock car racing, was elected vice president and general manager. Other charter officers and board members included publicity director Earl Kelley, a newspaper sports reporter from nearby Concord; popular entertainer Jerry Ball; Charles Crutchfield, general manager of three television stations; and A. C. Goines, G. B. Nalley, and G. D. Smith, all prominent business executives in North and South Carolina.

The groundbreaking ceremony for the site was held on July 29, 1959. Present on that hot, humid day were various dignitaries, including Lt. Gov. Luther E. Barnhardt of Concord. The reigning Miss Southern 500, Carolyn Melton of Cheraw, used a small gold shovel to turn the first spade of dirt. Construction of Charlotte Motor Speedway was finally under way.

The first order of business was to raise funds to build the Speedway. Financing was secured by selling

300,000 shares of stock for $1 a share. Turner and his associates experienced difficulty in moving the stock, and capital was only trickling in. Smith took the bull by the horns, bought radio and television ads, and embarked on a tireless sojourn throughout the state. Within days, he had sold 100,000 shares. Emboldened by the optimism, the owners moved construction along swiftly, despite the fact that payments were going out more quickly than monies were coming in, and a two-year project would have to be completed in half the time.

Before the Speedway began to take shape, a series of problems began to surface—insufficient financing, a faulty core-drill report, problems with the Securities Exchange Commission (SEC), three severe winter snowstorms, and sluggish advance ticket sales.

The construction firm of W. Owen Flowe & Sons was contracted with to move a mountain of dirt and the underlying rock on the Speedway property for eighteen cents a yard. But following what Turner considered a faulty core-drill report, the costs escalated more than tenfold. A half-million yards of solid granite were found under the dirt, and it had to be blasted out. Turner said it cost $70,000 just getting through the first turn. "The whole thing cost a half-million dollars more than it should have," said Turner.

Paving 24-degree banked turns was quite a task in 1960. Huge tractors on the level top side of each turn anchored the paving equipment with a series of heavy chains and clamps. The delicate process began in early May and extended into mid-June. *CMS Archives*

During the early stages of construction, the tract of land that would eventually be Charlotte Motor Speedway appeared to be nothing more than a derelict patch of rough terrain. This photo was taken in February 1960, just four months before the inaugural event, and shows excavating in what would become the third turn of the mile-and-a-half track. *CMS Archives*

Racer emeritus and Speedway President Curtis Turner shakes hands with slender Tim Flock, two-time NASCAR Grand National Champion. Turner drove in the inaugural World 600 on June 19,1960, while Flock, in semi-retirement from active driving, assisted in editing the souvenir program. A year later, Turner and Flock were banned from NASCAR for life for their failed efforts in organizing the drivers in the Teamsters Union. *CMS Archives*

Tiger Tom Pistone, a 5'3", 130-pound bundle of dynamite, was one of NASCAR's hardest chargers in the late 1950s and early 1960s. The diminutive Italian was a rookie in 1959 and won twice in Grand National competition, but was ineligible for the top rookie award since he had previous experience in late-model competition in another sanctioning body. Pistone was one of the drivers to conduct test runs at Charlotte Motor Speedway in the spring of 1960. *CMS Archives*

Legal problems with the SEC surfaced when the solicitation of stock in the still-unincorporated project went out by mail and television broadcasts across state lines. The SEC put this practice to an immediate halt.

Despite the early travails, construction continued at an accelerated rate.

On September 22, 1959, Turner and Smith flew to Daytona Beach to sign contracts for the inaugural NASCAR Grand National event. The World 600, the longest event on the annual calendar, received NASCAR's blessings and the race date was scheduled for May 29, 1960. The race would carry posted awards of $100,000, the first six-digit purse in NASCAR history. Turner and Smith told NASCAR president Bill France, Sr., that the Charlotte Motor Speedway would be completed by May 1, 1960.

Advance ticket sales were first offered in December 1959, and requests were processed at the Speedway's main offices at Suite 108 in the Liberty Life Building in Charlotte. But by the time tickets were being circulated, construction was woefully behind schedule. By Christmas 1959, the first race was scarcely five months away yet there was little more than a huge mound of dirt where the grandstands would be built, and the general outline of the first turn was all that was recognizable.

In January 1960, the management team erected light poles so construction crews could work around the clock in two 12-hour shifts. Meanwhile, Turner and Smith announced that advance ticket sales had been received from seven states: both Carolinas, Virginia, Pennsylvania, Maryland, Tennessee, and Indiana.

But advance ticket sales were lagging far below expectations. The Speedway's immediate savior became Bruton Smith, one of the new breed of auto racing promoters, a trend-setter who had a supercharged blend of infinite promotional skills and the ability to charm prospective clients. The tools of the promotional trade are only as important as the artist who uses them, and Smith had always been a master craftsman.

In late January, he invited the public out to the Speedway property to see for themselves the progress of the huge facility. He scheduled an open house on January 30 and 31, 1960. Turnout was terrific. "Our open house was far more successful than we anticipated," Smith reported. "Several thousand people showed up. We were busy both days selling reserved grandstand tickets, passing out informational brochures, and answering hundreds of questions about construction."

The open house observance stimulated ticket sales, and the practice was continued each weekend throughout the spring. The entire community was talking about Charlotte Motor Speedway and the upcoming World 600. Interested observers came out every day of the week, prompting contractors to make a public appeal that visitors to the Speedway site should not drive onto the property except during open house hours.

But there was a surprise in the spring package that was neither expected nor bargained for—three debilitating record snowfalls in three weeks. A blizzard the first weekend in March dropped 11 inches of snowfall throughout the Carolinas. It was one of the most powerful storms to hit the South since the turn of the century. It forced postponement of the 100-mile Grand National event at Smith's half-mile dirt Concord Speedway, and it brought a halt to all construction activity at Charlotte Motor Speedway.

Two more blasts of winter wonderland the following two weeks canceled Grand National events at Hillsboro and Richmond, and for a solid month construction work at the new Speedway was at a virtual standstill. As of mid-April, no concrete grandstands had been put into place, the massive project of paving the 1.5-mile track had not yet begun, no guard rails were in place, no garage stalls had been erected, and the control tower for officials and the press box were merely in the planning stages.

Ten days before the Memorial Day holiday weekend, Turner and Smith announced that the inaugural running of the World 600 would have to be postponed in order to complete the project. The only opening slot in the cramped NASCAR Grand National schedule was June 19. To get everything in place in just three weeks would be a daunting task.

With the cooperation of the weatherman and a herculean effort by all parties, Charlotte Motor Speedway was on the verge of being completed within hours of the first scheduled practice sessions. Only one small strip of pavement along the homestretch had not been paved when contractor W. Owen Flowe halted all work at the eleventh hour, demanding outstanding payments.

The turn of events that followed were "reminiscent of Ye Old Western Days," according to Dr. D. L. Morris, who chronicled Turner's life in *Timber on the Moon*, a 1966 paperback. Flowe ordered his staff to halt all work immediately and placed nearly three dozen bulldozers and earthmoving machines on the short strip of unpaved track with operators aboard who refused to move the equipment.

According to Dr. Morris, Turner sought the assistance of a local sheriff and attorney, both of whom stated that the dispute was on private property and if invaded, Turner had the right to protect it. The impasse ended only when Flowe's workers were marched away from their machines at gunpoint.

"The sight of shotguns and a revolver had an instantaneous effect," Dr. Morris wrote. "The drivers and operators lined up against the grandstand, hands up, sullenly silent while Curtis' brother Darnell and

A Tale of Two Tracks

Within a span of about 12 hours, celebrated racer Curtis Turner and short-track promoter Bruton Smith both made public announcements about their plans to build a high-banked paved superspeedway in the Charlotte area.

In April 1959, Turner and a small group of business associates announced their plans to build a mile-and-a-half plant on Highway 49, north of Charlotte. A few hours later, Smith said he was going to build a 2-mile track in Pineville, south of Charlotte.

Original plans by Turner and Smith varied greatly. Turner's plans included provisions for 45,000 grandstand seats and the possibility of a 1-mile road course in the infield for sports cars. Total expenditure on his project was estimated at $750,000. Turner planned to name his track Charlotte Motor Speedway.

Smith had ideas of a more elaborate plant that would feature a seating capacity of 75,000 with double-decked grandstands on the front chute and a single-level structure along the backstretch. Smith also envisioned a championship-caliber road course in the infield and a football field in the area between the grandstands and pit road. Cost for his Charlotte International Speedway would top $2 million.

Turner planned to stage a 500-mile NASCAR Grand National race while Smith wanted a 600-mile stock car race, a 12-hour contest for sports cars, and an Indianapolis-type car race or a big NASCAR Modified show.

Initially, Turner expressed a desire to proceed with his plans without Smith. "We won't work together on this," Turner told newspaper reporters on April 22, 1959. "And regardless of what he [Smith] does, we plan to go ahead with our plans. If he builds, too, it looks as if Charlotte will have two tracks."

Smith was of the opinion that a merger would be best for all parties. "I feel sure Turner and I can have a meeting on this thing soon," Smith told reporters. "I'd like to have Curtis throw in with me. He's a good man. Fact is, I'd like to see him as president of this thing."

Eventually, Turner and Smith pooled their efforts. The site for the tremendous project was moved from the Arrowood Industrial site on U.S. Highway 49 to a 550-acre piece of farmland that belonged to John Crossland, Jr., located in Cabarrus County, 12 miles north of Charlotte. An option on the desolate property was exercised in early May of 1959 and actual construction of Charlotte Motor Speedway began in July.

friend Acey Janey shorted the wires on the monstrous Caterpillar Tractor D9 and with (race car driver) Bob Welborn at the controls, pushed the other equipment off the track. Lights and armed guards were set up for the night. Next morning, the paving was finished and the track was completed."

In less than eleven months, Charlotte Motor Speedway emerged from a rock pile and a flickering thought to a brilliant reality. John B. Lippard, the landscape architect and site planner for the project, remarked, "I'll never see anything like this again, not in one lifetime. The building of Charlotte Motor Speedway has left me with one thought: If this can be done, and it has, anything under the sun is possible."

Tapestry of Terror

THE 1960 WORLD 600

The founders of Charlotte Motor Speedway cleared innumerable obstacles, and in 11 months the facility was ready to be host to its first competitive event. Curtis Turner and Bruton Smith had the vision and the courage to tackle an impossible project, and to them must go the honor of creating one of America's most exciting and improbable spectacles.

During the final stages of construction, Smith had been out hustling lap leader awards. He was able to persuade several area merchants and contingency firms to post $10 for each of the 400 laps, raising the total posted awards to $107,775, an all-time NASCAR record at the time.

Patterned after the Indianapolis 500 and Darlington's Southern 500, the first World 600 featured a three-abreast starting lineup. Fireball Roberts, Jack Smith, and Curtis Turner are on the front row moments before the command to fire the engines. This was the only event in Charlotte Motor Speedway history in which three cars started in each row. *CMS Archives*

Charlotte Motor Speedway president Curtis Turner didn't let his status as a speedway executive curb his appetite for high speed. Saddled up in his Holman-Moody Ford in preparation for the first World 600, Turner was regarded as one of the favorites in the inaugural event. Turner had announced the first of his many retirements in the summer of 1959 due to a nagging back injury. The 1960 World 600 was only his eighth appearance in a race since June of 1959. *CMS Archives*

A smattering of spectators turned out for the first practice sessions on Wednesday, June 15, 1960. Drivers toured the mile-and-a-half track for the first time, searching for the quickest groove. Nearly 70 cars checked in, hoping to earn a spot in the 60-car field. *CMS Archives*

The World 600 field was open to the 60 fastest Grand National cars. Practice sessions for the inaugural World 600 got under way on Wednesday, June 15. A crowd of 4,000 sat in the freshly poured concrete grandstands to watch the initial shakedown exercise.

The weather was seasonably warm and the freshly laid asphalt was unable to take the pounding from the heavy Grand National artillery. In less than an hour, a gash appeared in the pavement in the second turn. Later in the day, cracks and holes appeared throughout the third and fourth turns. After the session ended, repair crews began working on the track surface.

The following day, the mood was apprehensive in the garage area. Additional practice sessions and the run for the pole were scheduled. In the morning practice, the track broke up again. Repair crews swept off the chunks of broken pavement and did another round of patchwork on the track surface so that qualifying could proceed on schedule. Fireball Roberts, wheeling Smokey Yunick's fleet Pontiac, bagged the pole with a four-lap average of 133.904 miles per hour. Jack Smith's Pontiac and a Ford manned by Curtis Turner joined Roberts on the front row.

By the end of the day, the track was in shambles. "You could have half-hidden a big Chevrolet Impala in some of those holes," remarked two-time Grand National champion Buck Baker. Debris was swept off the corners and patching crews worked past dark in an effort to rectify the serious problems.

"When we left the track after that first day of qualifying," Baker recalled years later, "we didn't know what to expect when we came back the next day. We

During the first day of practice for the inaugural World 600, the freshly laid asphalt broke up badly in the turns. Cracked and broken chunks of pavement had to be swept off the track by repair crews, some of whom seemed completely in awe of the task at hand. *CMS Archives*

Glenn "Fireball" Roberts, arguably NASCAR's first superstar, wheeled Smokey Yunick's 1960 Pontiac to the pole position for the inaugural World 600. Unlike today's streamlined qualifying procedure, time trials on the superspeedways in NASCAR's early days consisted of a four-lap race against the clock with the average speed as the official qualifying record. Roberts ran one lap at 134.429 miles per hour and turned in a 133.904 miles per hour average to earn the inside front row starting position. *CMS Archives*

had run races on half-mile dirt tracks that were badly rutted, but speeds on those tracks were 50 to 60 miles per hour. This was a superspeedway where speeds were twice that fast. Still, we all wanted to run the 600. That purse was over $100,000—the most money we'd ever run for."

Jim Foster, a sports reporter for the *Spartanburg Herald* who would later be president of Daytona International Speedway, rode around the broken battlefield in a passenger car with Jack Smith after the day's activities. "Jack coaxed me into riding around the track with him," said Foster. "There were at least four big holes in the second turn and all of turns three and four were cracking. I didn't think there was any way 600 miles could be run on that track."

Once the patching was complete, Bruton Smith instructed track crews to drive all available dump trucks around the track in an effort to pack down the pavement and secure the surface. This procedure continued every evening, and paving crews attempted to patch the track throughout the week, including race morning. "The weather was so hot at the time," Smith recalled, "the asphalt was soft and pliable. Nobody, including

Curtis Turner and Bruton Smith, founders of Charlotte Motor Speedway, expressed anxiety when the track surface was ripped apart during initial practice runs. There was deep concern that the inaugural World 600 would be unable to go on as scheduled, but the track was patched well enough, and the race went into the record books on June 19, 1960. *CMS Archives*

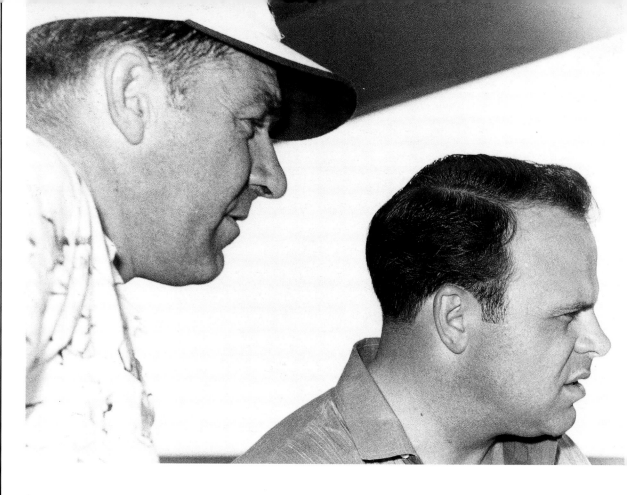

The turns at Charlotte Motor Speedway sat atop a huge mound of dirt that was excavated from the infield and surrounding parking lots. Little landscaping had been done when the first World 600 was run on June 19, 1960. "We got a view of the high banks on the third and fourth turn from the top side," wrote reporter Jim Foster of the *Spartanburg Herald* a few days before the inaugural race. "It is a straight drop of 130 feet. It will be suicide for any driver that goes over." *CMS photo by T. Taylor Warren*

Despite the three-week postponement and dire conditions that existed during qualifying, most of the front stretch grandstand seats were filled when the first World 600 got under way. Reserved seats along the front chute ranged from $8 to $15, with backstretch grandstand seating as low as $6. Infield admission to the inaugural event was $5. *CMS photo by T. Taylor Warren*

Lee Petty: Back to Choppin' Wood?

At the driver's meeting prior to the inaugural World 600, NASCAR executive manager Pat Purcell and competition director Norris Friel instructed the competitors to keep off the infield area, which separated pit road from the dogleg homestretch. No grass had been planted and NASCAR officials were fearful of a blinding dust storm if any cars cut across the dirt to enter the pit area.

Early in the race, Junior Johnson lost control of his Pontiac coming off the fourth turn. His car skidded into the dusty infield area and plowed into the Victory Circle structure, which had been placed on the edge of pit road. Johnson's errant car ripped out 30 feet of chain-link fence surrounding the temporary structure. He stopped in his pit and his crew made repairs. Johnson got back into the running and completed 287 laps before retiring with mechanical problems.

"Not long after that, I spun out in the same area," said Lee Petty. "With all the dust swirling around, I couldn't see. When I finally open my eyes, I had stopped right in my pit area. That was a stroke of luck, or so I thought. My boys checked everything over and I was on my way. Finished fifth."

Petty actually slid just past his pit area. He then drove his dust-covered Plymouth up pit road the wrong way to his pit stall. The crew serviced the car and Lee whipped a quick U-turn on pit road and continued in the race.

A few days after the race, NASCAR disqualified six drivers who had cut across the dusty infield, placing them at the bottom of the finishing order with no winnings. "The disqualification of six drivers in the World 600 NASCAR-sanctioned late model stock car race at Charlotte Motor Speedway, June 19, was upheld by Pat Purcell, executive manager of NASCAR," read a press release from the sanctioning body's Daytona Beach headquarters. "Purcell pointed out that the violated rule, which requires entering the pits properly, had been enforced in prior races at Daytona International Speedway. The six drivers were disqualified because they cut across the infield to their pits rather than enter by the pit road as instructed prior to the race. Friel told the drivers they would be disqualified if they entered the pit area by any route other than the pit road."

"It was three, four, maybe five days later when NASCAR told me I had been disqualified from the 600," the senior Petty said. "They disqualified a whole bunch of us. Really, what was I supposed to do, having spun out like that? I told NASCAR that if they were going to take my points and my money away, I might as well go back to choppin' wood for a living."

me, knew what to do about it. I ran trucks over it six hours to pack it. What I should have done was cool it with water."

When the garage opened on race morning, virtually all the cars were equipped with protective screens to guard against flying asphalt and debris. "Each car looked like a chicken coop was in front of it," said Bill Kiser, a sports reporter for the *Concord Tribune* who would later become public relations director at Darlington Raceway. "The drivers went out and bought screens, mud flaps, anything to protect their cars, especially the grilles and windshields."

Lee Petty, locked in a tight battle with his son Richard and Rex White for the 1960 NASCAR Grand National point lead, prepared his three-car team of Ply-

mouths with a variety of protective devices. "We knew the track wouldn't hold up for 600 miles with 60 cars on the track," said the patriarch of the Petty clan. "Heck, it wasn't holding up for four laps while one car qualified. We put big screens over the grill to keep flying rocks out of the radiators. We were hoping it would keep flying objects out of the driver's compartment, too. We didn't have any of those window nets like you see today. We even put rear tire flaps on our cars to keep debris from flying up into the guy behind us."

The drivers in the field for the inaugural World 600 were men with a common and dangerous trade, and those particular individuals welded themselves into a tight-knit, exclusive fraternity—the fraternity of courage.

Despite the dire predictions and opinions of several inside observers that the race would never run the full 600 miles, the much-anticipated event got under way shortly past 12:30 p.m. with a trackside audience of 35,462 on hand.

Borrowing the time-honored format from the Indianapolis 500, cars lined up three abreast for the 12:30 p.m. start on Sunday, June 19, 1960, which just happened to be the 11th anniversary of the birth of NASCAR's flagship series.

Fireball Roberts bolted from the pole position and led the opening lap. In the seventh lap, rookie Johnny Wolford lost control of his Ford as the leaders were bearing down in a speedy, noisy formation. Wolford slid onto the apron, then darted back onto the banking. The cluster of race leaders escaped unscathed, but Wolford was clobbered by Johnny Allen and Cotton Owens. Wolford, whose car burst into flames, was badly shaken but uninjured. All three cars were eliminated from competition.

Roberts held the lead through the first 65 laps when the first scheduled pit stops began. Tom Pistone, Junior Johnson, and Curtis Turner led for small stretches before Jack Smith assumed command in his Pontiac. By the halfway point, Smith had stretched his lead appreciably and lapped the field twice.

As Smith galloped into a huge lead, a number of favorites had retired, their mounts unable to tolerate the rough terrain. Roberts popped a tire on a piece of debris and crashed after 191 laps. Turner led twice for 21 laps but blew the engine in his Ford while running third. Joe Weatherly and Ned Jarrett, both destined to become two-time NASCAR champions, were each the victim of bouts with the retaining barrier following tire failures. Weatherly nearly broke through the steel rail in his mishap, ripping three sturdy support posts out of the ground and greatly bowing out the guard rail. Pistone, the little dynamo who led twice for 14 laps, departed

Rookie David Pearson, No. 67, leads Charley Griffith, No. 78, and eventual winner Joe Lee Johnson along the homestretch in the inaugural World 600 at Charlotte Motor Speedway. Although the grandstands contained several empty seats, the announced attendance was pegged at 78,000. Crowd estimates were later trimmed to 50,000 when the newspaper reporters in the press box didn't believe the first figure. Actual paid attendance, according to accounting records, was 35,462. *CMS photo by T. Taylor Warren*

with a severed brake line. Jim Reed, who had won Darlington's Southern 500 in 1959, crashed his Ford in a bone-jarring accident. Fred Lorenzen, the United States Auto Club (USAC) stock car champion who was just beginning to make a name for himself in NASCAR, fell out with engine problems. Marvin Panch, Speedy Thompson, Emanuel Zervakis, and Larry Frank were other top contenders who failed to go the distance.

As the marathon stretched into the shadows of the day, Smith had built an insurmountable five-lap lead. As he cruised toward the checkered flag, fate intervened. A sharp piece of metal sliced a gaping hole in his fuel tank, and the car spewed a trail of gasoline in its wake. Smith, hooked up with one of the first two-way radios in big-league NASCAR competition, pitted when he was called in by crew chief Bud Moore. Moore, who would form his own team a year later, and lead mechanic Pop Eargle tried a makeshift patching job with rags that took a three-lap bite out of Smith's lead. Returning to the track, Smith held a two-lap advantage

The Petty Engineering stable out of Level Cross, N.C., entered three electric-blue Plymouths in the first World 600. Lee Petty, who had won the NASCAR Grand National title three of the previous six years including 1958 and 1959, was in his familiar No. 42. Bobby Johns accepted a one-shot offer from Papa Lee and drove the No. 46, while 22-year-old Richard Petty was seated in the No. 43. All of the Petty cars finished in the top five, with Johns securing third after two spinouts. Richard ran fourth and Lee was fifth prior to their disqualifications. *CMS Archives*

Jack Smith had driven his No. 47 Pontiac into a huge five-lap lead late in the 1960 World 600 only to lose the race when a piece of shrapnel pierced his fuel tank. The misfortune relegated Smith to a 12th-place finish in the field of 60. Two weeks later, Smith scored his first and only superspeedway victory in the Firecracker 250 at Daytona. *CMS photo by T. Taylor Warren*

Without a blade of grass in the infield area between pit road and the front stretch, NASCAR officials warned drivers prior to the first World 600 that cutting across the dirt would result in disqualification. Six drivers— Lee Petty, Richard Petty, Junior Johnson, Bob Welborn, Paul Lewis, and Lenny Page—all stopped for pit stops after driving onto the dirt area, kicking up a dust storm. Most of the drivers had experienced some sort of problems during their adventurous route into the pits. Citing safety measures, NASCAR officials disqualified all six drivers and placed them at the bottom of the finishing order without points or winnings. *CMS photo by T. Taylor Warren*

over Joe Lee Johnson, who was taking his maiden voyage in a Chevrolet groomed by future Hall of Fame mechanic and team owner Paul McDuffie. Smith only ran a couple laps before he was black-flagged by starter Roby Combs. He limped to the pits once again. After another futile effort to make repairs, Smith pulled his Pontiac behind the pit wall, out of the race after leading for 198 laps.

"Most disappointing experience I ever had in my career," said Smith, who won 21 NASCAR Grand National races during his career, which ran from 1949 to 1964. "We had that race won. At first we thought a chunk of pavement bounced up and tore the gas tank. But later, Bud determined that it was something sharp that ripped into the tank. Bud thought it was a bumper guard off some T-Bird. We couldn't fix it. We tried stuffing rags and bars of soap into that hole. Nothing worked. We were done."

Joe Lee Johnson, a tough, whip-thin Tennessean who had won NASCAR's Convertible Series championship in 1959, led the rest of the way and finished four full laps ahead of runner-up Johnny Beauchamp, who had relief help from Johnny Allen. Johnson snared the $27,150 first prize for winning Charlotte Motor Speedway's inaugural World 600. Only 24 cars in the starting field of 60 were running at the finish. A myriad of wrecks and caution flags reduced the average speed to 107.735 miles per hour. Johnson had delicately threaded his way through the maze of broken pavement and shrapnel from crashed race cars to post the biggest win of his career.

"Paul McDuffie, who had been with Fireball Roberts in 1958 when he had such a good year (six wins in 10 starts on the Grand National trail), had just formed his own team before the 600," said Johnson, who started 20th on the grid. "The World 600 was our first race together. We knew the track would break up, so Paul's strategy was to find a comfortable pace and try to stay out of trouble. We ran a conservative pace, had good pit stops, and moved up when others ran into trouble. We didn't know we could win the race. When Jack fell out, we maintained out steady pace and brought it home."

Behind Johnson and Beauchamp were the three Petty Enterprises Plymouth entries driven by Bobby

Joe Lee Johnson poses beside his 1960 Chevrolet after the Victory Lane ceremonies on June 19, 1960. The Chattanooga, Tennessee, driver won $27,150 for his victory ride, which was more than half of his career earnings in NASCAR Grand National competition to that point. Note the windshield has been shattered by a piece of debris, and no explanation can be made for the brass automobile ornament that rests upside down on the trophy. *CMS photo by T. Taylor Warren*

Johns and Richard and Lee Petty. Johns, who lost the Daytona 500 in the final laps when he spun off the second turn while driving a Pontiac from the Smokey Yunick stable, survived two spin-outs to salvage third place in the 600. Later, Richard and Lee Petty were disqualified along with Junior Johnson, Paul Lewis, Bob Welborn, and Lenny Page for making improper pit stops. The rash of disqualifications moved rookie Gerald Duke and veteran Buck Baker into fourth and fifth places, respectively. Baker had been running in second place with 60 laps remaining when a broken ball joint on his Chevrolet forced him to the pits for time consuming repairs.

The race took more than five and a half hours to complete, and it acquired a survival-of-the-fittest profile minutes after the green flag. Artistically, the event contained frayed edges. But the fact the 600 was run at all was a miracle in itself.

Gross income for the inaugural World 600, including revenues from practice and qualifying days, totaled $304,694. With creditors figuratively lined up at the Charlotte Motor Speedway offices and demanding payments nearing $1 million, the management faced the prospect of an uphill struggle to solvency.

Winner Joe Lee Johnson hoists the handsome trophy in Victory Lane following his triumph in the 1960 World 600. Accompanying Johnson are Rita Souther, Miss Charlotte Motor Speedway, general manager Bruton Smith, and track president Curtis Turner. Johnson's "uniform" consisted of a pair of trousers and a Champion Spark Plug T-shirt. *CMS photo by T. Taylor Warren*

CHAPTER 3

Scaling the Jagged Financial Rocks

1960–1962

The second event at Charlotte Motor Speedway was the National 400, scheduled for October 16, 1960, with posted awards of $65,389. "We named the race the National 400 because in all probability it will determine the 1960 national championship of NASCAR's late model division," said General Manager Bruton Smith in a July 1960 press release.

The Speedway was open for tire tests the weekend before the 400. While the track had not been repaved following the debacle in June, the surface had received considerable attention and was proclaimed in good shape for the upcoming 400-miler. During the testing sessions, Tiger Tom Pistone blew a tire and crashed heavily in the first turn. Pistone barely missed adding his name to the black-bordered memorial pages of various racing publications. Miraculously, he escaped injury.

Bobby Johns and David Pearson, in a pair of Pontiacs, lead this high-speed chase into the first turn at the Speedway in the 1962 National 400. In the formative days of superspeedway racing, cars formed a wide groove in the corners, evident by the three-lane width of rubber laid down on the banking. The preferred line in the 1990s was directly on the bottom of the racetrack. *CMS Archives*

unfavorable publicity had a telling effect on the gate. Only 29,166 paid to attend the National 400, far below expectations.

Speedy Thompson prevailed in another wreck-strewn affair, giving the up-and-coming Wood Brothers Racing Team its first victory on a superspeedway. Fireball Roberts led most of the way but crashed after a tire failure. Lenny Page, one of the six drivers disqualified from the World 600, was seriously injured when his Thunderbird tagged the wall and was clobbered by Don O'Dell.

Rex White finished sixth in the 400 and clinched the 1960 NASCAR Grand National championship.

Gross receipts from the National 400 amounted to $188,832, which allowed the Speedway to net a modest profit. It wasn't, however, enough to appease all the creditors.

With debts soaring close to the million-dollar mark, the Charlotte Motor Speedway was being pressured to settle outstanding payments. In an effort to provide racing fans a variety of events and to increase revenue, the Speedway officials announced an ambitious 12-day schedule for May 1961. The festivities would include a pair of 100-mile qualifying races on the opening weekend, a

A neatly groomed garage stall greeted the NASCAR Grand National teams in October 1960, when they checked in for the inaugural National 400. Seven different makes of cars competed in the first National 400: Chevrolet (16), Ford (14), Plymouth (6), Pontiac (6), Thunderbird (4) (which was classified separately from Ford in 1960), Oldsmobile (2), and Dodge (2). *CMS photo by T. Taylor Warren*

Diminutive Rex White and lanky Richard Petty were locked in a battle for the 1960 NASCAR Grand National championship. Both were making their first concentrated efforts for the title, neither having run the full tour before in their careers. White finished sixth in the 1960 400-miler and clinched the championship. Petty ran second to race winner Speedy Thompson. *Daytona International Speedway Archives*

Rex White, who had all but wrapped up the 1960 NASCAR Grand National championship, was also participating in the tire tests. Following Pistone's mishap, White delivered a verbal blast about the track conditions. "If you ask me, the track stinks," said the stridently outspoken White. "I felt something like that would happen to Pistone. There was an excuse for the condition of the track for the World 600 back in June. Frankly, it's worse now than it ever was."

White's statements were widely reported in daily and racing newspapers, and Charlotte Motor Speedway was embroiled in another controversy.

NASCAR President Bill France, Sr., flew to Charlotte and inspected the track on Monday, October 10, two days before qualifications began. "The track is not dangerous," France asserted. "I'm sure that every driver out there has driven on tracks a lot worse. There are a couple of rough spots on the third turn, but I'm sure they can be smoothed out before race time."

Although the Charlotte Motor Speedway received France's endorsement, the

format strikingly similar to the annual Speedweeks in Daytona. Also on tap was a 100-mile event for NASCAR Modified and Sportsman cars the day before the 600.

Richard Petty nosed out Ralph Earnhardt to win the first 100-mile qualifier, and Joe Weatherly galloped past Junior Johnson with two laps remaining to snare the second race win. Petty and Weatherly would start on the front row for the May 28 World 600.

Johnson drove the John Masoni–owned Pontiac groomed by the incomparable Ray Fox in the second 100-miler. Curiously, Johnson decided to step out of the Fox car for the 600. "I drove Ray's car in the qualifying race because he didn't have a driver," said Johnson, one of NASCAR's early lords of speed. "I was going to drive for Rex Lovette's Holly Farms team in the 600, which was my regular ride. We didn't want to run the risk of tearing up our good car in the qualifier, so Bobby Isaac drove my car one lap and parked it. I didn't really get out of Fox's car for the 600, I just got in it for the qualifier."

David Pearson, the 1960 Grand National Rookie of the Year, had not entered the World 600 due to lack of funds for his independent operation. The dual adventure of being owner and driver had taken its toll financially. Fox offered Pearson a ride at the eleventh hour. "I needed a driver and I had seen David doing some pretty good things in that tired iron of his," said Fox. "I figured he deserved a chance in some good equipment. Besides, Cotton Owens and Bud Moore spoke very highly of David."

The first thing an exciting wildcat racer must have is a willing disregard for all the consequences. Pearson stepped into the Fox machine and immediately established himself as a firm contender in the 600. "After we went out for a practice run," remarked Pearson, "Ray asked me how the car felt. I didn't know how a strong car should feel. I told him it must be OK. We were runnin' fast and kept it off the wall, so it must have been a good-handling race car."

Pearson qualified at a record 138.381 miles per hour and started third, behind twin 100 winners Petty and Weatherly.

Pearson's first effort with a strong team was surprisingly propitious. He dominated the race, leading six times for 225 laps. Fate nearly snatched victory from his grasp, however, when a tire blew with two miles remaining. Rather than pitting, Pearson soldiered on, crossing the finish line on three wheels and a shower of sparks from the bare right rear rim. Having a propensity to learn quickly, Pearson followed the 600 triumph with victories at Daytona and Atlanta, claiming his rightful position as one of NASCAR's finest and a

Following repeated criticism about the Charlotte Motor Speedway, NASCAR president Bill France, Sr., personally inspected the track surface in October 1960. France is joined by Ralph Moody of the famed Holman-Moody Ford team. France declared that the track was "not dangerous" and the inaugural National 400 was flagged off on October 16, 1960. *CMS Archives*

Lenny Page of Buffalo, New York, was seriously injured in a grinding crash during the 1960 National 400. Chris Economaki, taking photographs for *National Speed Sport News*, rushed to the aid of the unconscious Page and most likely saved his life. "I tended to a deep cut in his neck," said Economaki, "and assisted the medical crew when they got there. After Page recovered from his injuries, I got a nice letter from him, thanking me for saving his life." *CMS Archives*

future legend. A crowd of 45,538 watched one of the classic upsets in NASCAR history.

Gross revenue for the month was $382,091. Charlotte Motor Speedway was well on its way to solvency, but not fast enough to satisfy the creditors.

On Thursday, June 8, 1961, 11 days after the second World 600, Curtis Turner and Bruton Smith resigned from Charlotte Motor Speedway in a "stormy" board of directors meeting. Neither Turner nor Smith salvaged any position of authority from the upheaval, although Smith was retained as a promotional director.

In a last-ditch effort to provide funding to save the track, Turner approached the Teamsters Union about obtaining an $850,000 loan. In return, the flamboyant driver would attempt to organize a driver's union and

introduce pari-mutuel betting on Grand National events. NASCAR President Bill France, Sr., upon hearing Turner's intent to unionize the drivers, promptly banned Turner from all NASCAR races for life, along with Tim Flock, who remained by Turner's side throughout the entire ordeal.

Turner and Flock filed a lawsuit against NASCAR, but the case was thrown out of court. It was ruled that the Teamsters could not legally make a loan to a company it was attempting to organize.

Allen Nance, a 38-year-old building contractor, was temporarily elevated to the president's chair at the Speedway. C. D. "Duke" Ellington, a 32-year-old attorney who specialized in finances, was appointed executive vice president of the Charlotte Motor Speedway.

The 1961 National 400 attracted 35,821 spectators for the second annual running of the autumn event, an entertaining affair won by Joe Weatherly in a close decision over Richard Petty. Two weeks later, the Speedway was scheduled to go onto the auction block, an action brought on by several creditors who had filed liens approaching $1 million against the struggling facility. Action by the track's management was successful in stalling the foreclosure sale for 30 days.

Speedway management went into Federal District Court under an obscure law that allowed the court to virtually take over the Speedway and direct its management to reorganize or take any necessary steps to get the corporation back on its feet. Charlotte Motor Speedway almost became a ward of the court. The State Superior Court, which had ordered the foreclosure sale, was overruled.

Jimmy Thompson and Bill DeCoster led the field on the pace lap for the 100-mile NASCAR Modified event at the speedway in May 1961. The event attracted only a couple thousand spectators. DeCoster won the 67-lap race in his 1957 Ford powered by a 1959 engine, three two-barrel carburetors, and a three-speed floor shift. *CMS photo by T. Taylor Warren*

Federal District Judge J. B. Craven, Jr., extended the corporate life of Charlotte Motor Speedway on Friday, December 8, 1961, placing the track under Chapter X of the Federal Bankruptcy Act. Jack T. Hamilton, attorney for the stockholders' committee, told the court that a pair of Washington, D.C., financiers, Henry S. Morgan and James S. McIlvaine, had agreed to put up $300,000 to help keep the Speedway afloat, provided stockholders matched the loan.

In denying the creditors' motion to foreclose, Judge Craven said, "The evidence presented here today convinces me there is almost a probability that new money will come in to make it possible to pay off the secured creditors." He appointed Robert N. "Red" Robinson as trustee in reorganization, and he was given until March 1962 to come up with a plan to satisfy creditors.

As the deadline approached, a special committee meeting was spearheaded by A. C. Goines and Richard Howard, two prominent Speedway stockholders. Having already raised $254,000, they were still $46,000 shy of the funds needed to thwart certain foreclosure. With about 100 stockholders present in the auditorium of the Esso Building at Park Road Shopping Center in Charlotte, Howard, then a Denver, North Carolina, furniture dealer, stood up and shouted, "Let's get started. Here is $5,000."

Within two hours, the stockholders had contributed enough money to bring the total to $301,510. Charlotte Motor Speedway was blessed with another extension and preparation began immediately for the 1962 season.

Ralph Earnhardt, driver for the Cotton Owens–owned Pontiac team in 1961, was among the favorites in the 1961 World 600. Earnhardt finished second to Richard Petty in the 100-mile qualifying race, equaling his best finish in NASCAR Grand National competition. Earnhardt drove in 51 big league NASCAR events in his career, earning one pole and 16 top-10 finishes. *CMS Archives*

The 100-mile qualifying races at Charlotte in 1961 carried championship points and therefore were regarded as official NASCAR Grand National events. Richard Petty wheeled his No. 43 Plymouth to victory in the first of the two twin 100s. It was the fifth of 200 career victories for Petty. *CMS Archives*

David Pearson limps across the finish line barely traveling 50 miles per hour at the conclusion of the 1961 World 600. Taking his first ride in competitive equipment, Pearson built up a three-lap cushion when the right rear tire blew with just over a lap remaining. He still won the race by two full laps. *CMS Archives*

Replacing the 100-mile qualifiers for the spring race were a pair of 50-milers with no championship points. Fireball Roberts and David Pearson won the sprint races and earned starting spots on the front row for the 600. Having secured the top seven starting positions, Pontiacs were heavily favored in the third annual World 600.

Pontiacs dominated the race, but another dark horse would grace Victory Lane. Nelson Stacy, a 41-year-old refugee from the Midwestern dirt tracks, came from his 18th starting position to win the 600. Driving a Holman-Moody Ford, Stacy took the lead just eight laps from the finish when leader Pearson blew an engine while holding a lap lead. Pearson was seeking his second straight victory in the 600-mile marathon but had not won a Grand National event since September 1961.

Stacy had become one of NASCAR's most unlikely phenoms. Drifting out of Cincinnati in the twilight of his career, he landed a ride in NASCAR and won the

David Pearson engineered a stunning upset in the 1961 World 600, driving Ray Fox's Pontiac to a decisive victory. It was the first of 105 NASCAR Winston Cup (then Grand National) wins for the Spartanburg, South Carolina, sophomore. Sharing the Victory Lane ceremonies are perky Nancy Ann Harrison and voluptuous Hollywood starlet June Wilkinson. *CMS Archives*

Fireball Roberts had led 107 of the first 113 laps in the 1961 National 400 when his Pontiac suddenly lost power exiting the fourth turn. Roberts' disabled car was hit squarely from behind by Bill Morgan. White paint from Morgan's Ford was clearly visible on the back of Fireball's bucket seat. "I picked glass from my neck and back for two weeks," Roberts said after the horrendous crash. *CMS photo by T. Taylor Warren*

Ned Jarrett (No. 11) and Darel Dieringer (No. 90) battle side by side in the 1962 World 600. Following closely are Herb Tillman (No. 91) and Tiny Lund (No. 30). Dieringer and Tillman were in twin Dodges prepared by Bob Osiecki (pronounced Oh-SEE-kee), an immensely talented mechanic whose background was in drag racing. In 1962, Osiecki entered 16 NASCAR Grand National events with six different drivers. *CMS Archives*

1961 Darlington Southern 500 as a rookie. Durable as cured leather, Stacy won the Rebel 300 at Darlington in a near photo finish over Marvin Panch two weeks before the 600.

Stacy had been hardly considered a favorite at Charlotte. He had been ticketed to drive a Ford Galaxie with a new "fastback" roof. The sleek roofline was a new aerodynamic feature fresh from Dearborn designed specifically for the high-banked superspeedways. However, on the eve of qualifications, NASCAR refused to issue approval for the new roof since it had not been available to the public in mass production. Team owners John Holman and Ralph Moody hastily prepared backups for Stacy and lead driver Fred Lorenzen. Stacy led only 13 laps to post the third straight upset in the spring classic.

Race day temperatures hovered near 100 degrees. The sun hammered down like a white-hot sledge, and the crowd of 45,875 clustered sweatily in the grandstands for the 4-hour, 46-minute spectacle. Heat waves shimmered off the pavement, but the track held up well. The gremlins that had haunted the track surface the first two years were kept at bay despite the brutal heat.

The searing heat was blamed for a smaller-than-expected walk-up crowd, yet gross revenue for the week was $368,677. In a July 5, 1962, hearing in District Court, Red Robinson requested additional time to give stockholders a chance to reorganize. Judge Craven granted the extension. "It is my opinion that the Speedway will be successfully reorganized under Chapter X of

the Federal Bankruptcy Act. I am committing myself for the first time to see this thing through to the end," the judge said.

Richard Howard was able to secure a $345,000 loan to implement improvements at the Speedway. In September 1962, a new scoreboard went up, the steep ramps leading to the grandstands were paved, a new well was drilled to provide an adequate water supply to the restrooms, and sod was laid on the back sides of the banked turns to prevent erosion.

The third annual National 400, held on October 14, 1962, drew a healthy crowd of 40,211. Junior Johnson, who hooked up with Ray Fox after David Pearson left to join the Cotton Owens team, outran Fred Lorenzen and outlasted Marvin Panch to score his first victory of the season and his first superspeedway triumph since the 1960 Daytona 500. Charlotte Motor Speedway officials were pleased with the spectator turnout, which enabled them to net $97,266 from gross receipts of $281,348.

In two short years, Charlotte Motor Speedway had emerged from the jagged financial rocks of bankruptcy to the doorstep of solvency.

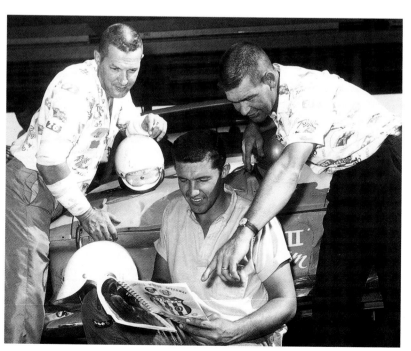

Nelson Stacy drove his Holman-Moody Ford to a surprising triumph in the 1962 World 600, his second superspeedway victory in three weeks. Stacy won three NASCAR Grand National events in 1962 but only drove in 14 races after his superlative season. CMS photo by Don Hunter

A youthful Richard Petty (kneeling) looks at the 1962 National 400 souvenir program as Speedy Thompson (right) points something out in the program. Jim Paschal looks on from the left. Petty, Thompson, and Paschal were drivers for the Petty Enterprises team in the 1962 400-miler. Paschal finished 6th, Thompson was 9th, and Petty came home 16th. CMS photo by T. Taylor Warren

Dynamic Duels and Dangerous Curves

1963–1966

Charlotte Motor Speedway, hampered by a series of financial setbacks from the day the first spade of dirt was turned, emerged from the Federal Bankruptcy Act and became a solvent corporation in April 1963. The Speedway paid off $740,376 to secured creditors of the track. A total of 20 creditors received payments ranging from a high of $356,294.14 all the way down to $55.97. Payments were made through the Cabarrus County Clerk, where lien judgments had been granted in Superior Court in 1960 and 1961. The remainder of the outstanding debts were paid off a few weeks later.

In the early 1960s, motor homes and campers were luxury items that rarely frequented the infield at NASCAR stock car races. Most of the occupants raised scaffolds in order to get a better view of the races. Tower grandstands along the outer rim of the track were non-existent as well. *CMS Archives*

Junior Johnson (No. 3) and Fred Lorenzen (No. 28) lead the first five rows on the pace lap just before the start of the 1963 World 600. The Holman-Moody team placed four of its factory-backed Fords in the top 10: Lorenzen, Fireball Roberts (starting fourth), Nelson Stacy (No. 29), and Jimmy Pardue (No. 0). Safety precautions for the media were not as strict as they are today as one lone photographer stands on the track near the opening in the inside retaining wall. *CMS photo by T. Taylor Warren*

New officers and directors were appointed by Judge J. B. Craven, who was in charge of the track's business during its tenure under Chapter X of the Federal Bankruptcy Act. A. C. Goines, one of the charter stockholders in the Charlotte Motor Speedway, was appointed as president by Judge Craven. Duke Ellington became executive vice president and Richard Howard was the new vice president and general manager.

"Automobile racing is soaring to the Everest of the sports world," Goines said in 1963. "Last year, it was the number-two spectator sport in the nation. I think that one day auto racing will take over as the most popular spectator sport in the world. We are gearing the Charlotte Motor Speedway toward that day."

While the Charlotte Motor Speedway made the headlines off the track in 1963, NASCAR drivers Fred Lorenzen, who possessed all the credentials to become a blue-chip professional racer, and Junior Johnson, an absolutely peerless gladiator in high-speed combat, were grabbing all the attention on NASCAR's high-banked speedways. Lorenzen was the flagship driver on Ford's almighty factory team while Johnson and team owner Ray Fox campaigned a Chevrolet without admitted factory support, admirably filling the role as underdogs.

Lorenzen's tactical awareness was uncanny, and in a short period of time he was universally recognized as one of the smartest drivers in the sport, with a rare ability to handle any situation that confronted him. He finished second to Tiny Lund in the 1963 Daytona 500, and rebounded in the next superspeedway event, winning the Atlanta 500. Johnson, on the other hand, was a thundering soldier of speed who had claimed the deed for the golden gates of the home of the brave. He had been swift in all the early season events, but rarely finished.

The 1963 World 600 pitted the crafty Lorenzen against the wild and adventurous Johnson. Fittingly, Johnson was on the pole with a record speed of 141.148 miles per hour. Lorenzen was just a tick behind at 141.111.

The fourth annual edition of the spring classic was postponed from its original May 26 race date until June 2 by heavy rain. All cars were impounded for a week. Despite the postponement, a record crowd of 58,722 spectators turned out to watch the highly anticipated event.

The huge throng was treated to a classic speed duel packed with drama. Lorenzen and Johnson forged to the front and battled ferociously for the entire 600 miles. Johnson led for a total of 289 laps and padded his lead to 16 seconds with 20 laps remaining.

Having a comfortable lead, Johnson slackened his pace. Lorenzen had closed the deficit to just under four seconds with three laps to go when the right rear tire of Johnson's Chevrolet blew out. Lorenzen sailed into the lead and crossed the finish line with an empty fuel tank. He won $27,780 from the $117,225 purse, pushing his season's earnings to $69,480.

Lorenzen's season was staggering. The all-time record for money winnings in a single NASCAR Grand National season was $70,742 established by Joe Weatherly in 1962, and that included post-season awards. Lorenzen was only a few dollars shy of the record in the first few days in June. He even ranked fourth in the point standings, despite competing in only 12 of the season's first 26 races.

Throughout the summer and early fall, Lorenzen went on a proverbial tear, finishing no lower than third in nine starts while winning three races. In early September, Lorenzen became the first driver to surpass $100,000 in single-season earnings.

Johnson performed the role of the rabbit, mounting huge leads only to have something go awry with victory in sight. He managed to win on the short tracks in Winston-Salem and Hickory but fell out of most of the other events.

Junior Johnson and team owner Ray Fox hoist armfuls of trophies following Johnson's triumph in the 1963 National 400. The triumph was the seventh of the 1963 season for the Fox-Johnson team, but it was their last victory with a Chevrolet. The potent team switched to Dodge in 1964, then parted company after a sluggish start. *CMS photo by T. Taylor Warren*

The stage was set for another Lorenzen-Johnson headlining battle when the Grand Nationals returned to Charlotte Motor Speedway for the fourth annual National 400. The intense rivalry between the two star drivers was a boost to ticket sales at Charlotte. An event record of 46,531 turned out in perfect weather to watch the race. For Junior Johnson and Ray Fox, it would be their final effort with Chevrolet. "We will not be running a Chevy next year," said team owner Fox. "General Motors has gotten out of racing. We've been having trouble getting enough parts to finish out this year. This is the last time around."

Johnson and Lorenzen qualified on the front row for the fourth time on a superspeedway in the 1963 season. Johnson dominated the race, leading 209 of the 267 laps. He finished 12 seconds ahead of Lorenzen and became the first driver to win more than one major race at the Charlotte track.

During the off-season, track officials authorized a stock-issue dividend—the first in the track's history—and announced plans to begin removal of a large rock-and-gravel mound in the infield. The hill had blocked the view of the second turn from the main grandstand since the speedway opened in 1960. Also new to the

Jimmy Pardue put his No. 54 Burton-Robinson Plymouth on the pole for the 1964 World 600 and led the opening 33 laps. Paul Goldsmith (No. 25) and Bobby Isaac (No. 26) give chase in their twin Nichels Engineering mounts. All three of the early front-runners encountered engine problems in the 600-mile marathon and failed to finish. *Chrysler Photographic Photo*

Speedway was the Ford Tower, a huge concrete structure located atop the grandstands near the first turn, offering a superlative view of the entire track. Track president A. C. Goines and general manager Richard Howard had taken a leaf from Bruton Smith's vision of having a double-decked grandstand.

The 1964 NASCAR Grand National season began on a tragic note. Two-time defending series champion Joe Weatherly lost his life in California's Riverside 500. Once the touring professionals returned to the high-banked superspeedways, it was clearly evident that the long-time underdog Plymouth and Dodge teams had closed the gap with the reintroduction of the hemispherical engine. The Hemi had been in Chrysler's bag of tricks since 1951 but had not been raced since 1956. Richard Petty led a 1-2-3 sweep for Plymouths in the Daytona 500. Speeds escalated at an alarming rate in 1964. Petty qualified 20 miles per hour faster at Daytona than he had in 1963.

When the tour came to Charlotte Motor Speedway for the fifth annual World 600, Jimmy Pardue, who finished second at Daytona, earned the pole with a speed of 144.346 miles per hour in his Plymouth. Junior Johnson, who left the Ray Fox Dodge team early in the year to join the Ford contingent with team owner Banjo Matthews, topped Pardue's

Charlotte Motor Speedway was the first major stock car racing facility to have a double-decked grandstand. Co-founder Bruton Smith had visions of tower grandstands as early as 1960. By the 1964 World 600, the huge Ford Tower concrete structure was ready, and it was quickly sold out for the first race.
CMS photo by T. Taylor Warren

Fireball Roberts' burning Ford lies upside down on the backstretch of Charlotte Motor Speedway after the eighth lap crash in the 1964 World 600. Roberts looped his car to avoid hitting two spinning cars and struck the edge of the concrete inside wall. The NASCAR icon was gravely injured and died six weeks later.
CMS Archives

speed a day later with a record run at better than 145 miles per hour.

An enthusiastic crowd of 66,311 turned out on a warm afternoon to watch the field of 44 take the green flag at 12:30 p.m. on Sunday, May 24, 1964. Just minutes after the start, a crash occurred on the backstretch that ultimately changed the landscape of NASCAR stock car racing and took the life of its most endearing hero.

Johnson and Ned Jarrett hooked bumpers in the eighth lap and slid down the backstretch. Fireball Roberts, in his second season with the Holman-Moody team, put his Ford into a slide to avoid directly hitting Johnson or Jarrett. Roberts' car struck an opening in the inside concrete wall with the rear of his car and exploded on impact. Gravely injured, he was airlifted by helicopter to Charlotte Memorial Hospital in extremely critical condition with burns over 80 percent of his body.

Jim Paschal, driving a Petty Enterprises Plymouth, went on to score a four-lap victory over teammate Richard Petty in the tragic 600. Rex White, who retired from Grand National competition a month later, finished third. Lorenzen, who entered the race on a personal five-race winning streak, was fourth and Billy Wade, Weatherly's replacement on the Bud Moore team, came home fifth.

Roberts gamely battled for his life against impossible odds while he lay in the hospital for 39 days. In late June, he developed a high fever and passed away on the morning of July 2, 1964, at the age of 35. The racing world mourned the loss of its most revered pilot.

The third and fourth turns had been repaved by the time the NASCAR Grand National tour returned for the October 18 National 400. But another top star was missing from the lineup. Jimmy Pardue suffered fatal injuries during a tire test at Charlotte Motor Speedway on September 22. His Plymouth blew a tire entering the third turn and plowed through the steel guard rail, uprooting the wooden support posts and tearing out 48 feet of railing. His car tumbled down the steep embankment into an empty parking lot.

The Midwestern Automobile Racing Club of America (ARCA) scheduled a 200-mile late-model race on Saturday as a support event to the National 400. Curtis Turner, exiled by NASCAR, was eligible to compete in the ARCA event. His entry was heavily promoted by new publicity director Bob Latford, who succeeded Earl Kelley in June.

Jim Paschal drove his Petty Enterprises Plymouth to a four-lap victory in the 1964 World 600 and earned a trip to Victory Lane on a superspeedway for the first time. Joining the 37-year-old veteran is his longtime girlfriend, Becky Rich. *CMS photo by T. Taylor Warren*

There was no speed limit on pit road at NASCAR tracks in 1964 and drivers would often engage in serious close-quarter racing on the narrow strip of pavement. Fred Lorenzen and Richard Petty—with two wheels in the grass—drag down pit lane during the 1964 National 400. *CMS photo by T. Taylor Warren*

Curtis Turner, Charlotte Motor Speedway's first president, was banned from NASCAR in 1961 after his failed attempts to organize the drivers into the Teamsters union. He was permitted to compete in the ARCA 200 at the Speedway he co-founded in 1964. Turner overpowered the field and won easily. In Victory Lane, Turner is joined by Pat Flannery, Miss ARCA. *CMS photo by T. Taylor Warren*

Jim Paschal (No. 41) and Dick Hutcherson collide in the fourth turn during the 1965 World 600. Paschal had been a victim of the Chrysler Corporation boycott in 1965 but was lured back into action by Charlotte Motor Speedway general manager Richard Howard. Paschal, the 1964 World 600 winner, was seated in a Chevrolet owned and prepared by Toy Bolton. *Charlotte Motor Speedway*

During qualifications, Richard Petty sped to a new track record with a blistering 150.711 miles per hour to earn the pole for the 400. Nobody could match Petty's brute speed as he led 188 of the 267 laps. But the crowd of 66,399 rose to its feet as Lorenzen closed in the final 10 laps. Petty and Lorenzen battled at breakneck speed during the final laps until the right front tire blew on Petty's Plymouth, sending him into the retaining barrier. "The tire just went," said Petty, who was badly bruised but uninjured in the crack-up. "I went the same route as Pardue did. I was lucky enough to stay inside the racetrack. I may be sore all over for the next few days, but all that's hurting me right now is my pocketbook."

Lorenzen coasted home the winner as the caution flag came out. "It was a shame the race ended the way it did," said Lorenzen, who led only seven laps en route to his second victory at Charlotte. "I'm just glad he didn't get hurt. I was lucky I won this one." Jim Paschal finished a lap back in second place. Petty's 265 laps completed was good enough for third place and it all but clinched the 1964 Grand National championship, his first of seven NASCAR titles.

The ARCA 200, rained out on Saturday, was rescheduled for Sunday, October 25. A modest crowd of 11,440 was on hand, and most of those people came to watch Turner run. He led 101 of the 134 laps and finished a lap ahead of the field. "Boy, it sure felt good to be back in the harness," said the Virginian. "It's a big thrill to win a big race on a track you built, even if you don't know the drivers you beat. They really have made a lot of improvements on the track since I was on it last. It's everything I ever dreamed it would be."

Turner wanted back in the NASCAR fold but knew his chances were slim that his lifetime ban would be lifted. "I'd come back tomorrow if the man in Daytona (Bill France, Sr.) gave me the sign. I haven't even tried to talk with him this year but did try several times last year without any success."

The 1965 NASCAR Grand National season was perhaps the most controversial on record. The element of danger had cut deeply into the vein of the sport in 1964, and Billy Wade had been killed in another tire test at Daytona in January. New specifications, designed to slow the cars and provide additional safety measures, took aim on the expensive limited-production engines. The powerful Chrysler Hemi was on the chopping block, as were the smaller Plymouth and Dodge models Chrysler had used in 1964. As a result, Chrysler yanked all of its factory-supported teams off the track.

When the season started, Richard Petty, David Pearson, and a host of other top names were on the

sidelines. Track promoters started taking heavy hits at the gate, and that was also the case at Charlotte. Barely 50,000 showed up for the sixth annual World 600 on May 23, 1965. Lorenzen edged upstart driver Earl Balmer by 6.4 seconds after the newcomer from Indiana made up four full laps in the final 200 miles.

By midseason, Bill France, Sr., had eased a number of the heavy restrictions placed on the Chrysler camp. The Plymouths and Dodges were permitted to run the short tracks, but the superspeedways were still off limits. Charlotte Motor Speedway executives Goines and Howard joined several track promoters in a meeting with France at Atlanta during the summer months. All voiced complaints about the lack of competition and the poor attendance, and pleaded with France to permit Curtis Turner to return to NASCAR racing.

By mid-August, Curtis Turner was back in NASCAR's good graces and was entered in a Wood Brothers Ford for the October 17, 1965, edition of the National 400. The sixth annual running of the autumn classic became one for the ages. Turner was magnificent in his first Grand National effort at Charlotte since 1961. Fred Lorenzen, Dick Hutcherson, A. J. Foyt, and Turner treated the audience of nearly 35,000 to a white-knuckle struggle and produced a series of images seemingly frozen in time—the epic three-abreast battle, interrupted only when Foyt grazed the wall and spun with six laps to go.

Lorenzen went on to nose out Hutcherson by three car lengths as Turner wound up third, his stride broken when he lifted to avoid hitting Foyt. "The duel was everything racing is supposed to be, and more," said award-winning journalist Benny Phillips. "Every person present was standing, waving, and shouting. It was one of the greatest duels the sport has ever known between two of the greatest drivers who ever answered the call to 'Gentlemen, Start Your Engines.' Lorenzen

won what could be considered the most spine-tingling race of his career, and he did it in spectacular fashion."

The race was marred, however, by the death of Harold Kite, whose car was pancaked in a multi-car accident in the second lap. Kite, who won the NASCAR Grand National event at Daytona in 1950, had ended a nine-year retirement in order to compete at Charlotte.

The first half of the 1966 season was again stained by a boycott—this time by Ford Motor Company, which withdrew its factory-backed cars in a dispute over a limited-production overhead cam engine. The result again was poor attendance and a lack of competition across the board, and promoters took it on the chin. Richard Howard was able to retrieve Ned Jarrett and Marvin Panch, two of Ford's top drivers, for the May 22, 1966, World 600. Howard was instrumental in lining Jarrett up with independent Ford team owner Henley Gray and Panch with the Petty Plymouth operation. It cost Howard a king's ransom to secure the services of Jarrett and Panch for the 600, both of whom were set to retire after the season.

A crowd of about 50,000 assembled in the grandstands, a surprisingly strong figure considering the unstable nature of the sport at that time. With the sands

The 1965 National 400 was perhaps the most electrifying duel in the history of the speedway. The lead was swapped repeatedly, and with six laps remaining, Dick Hutcherson (No. 29), Fred Lorenzen (No. 28), and A. J. Foyt (No. 41) were three abreast, battling for first place. Lorenzen prevailed in the intense struggle, his fourth triumph at Charlotte. *CMS Archives*

Marvin Panch (No. 42) sidestepped Ford's boycott in 1966 and hooked up with Petty Enterprises for the 1966 World 600. Panch, who had driven Fords most of his career, won the seventh annual running of the May classic in a year-old Plymouth with relief help from Richard Petty. Forty-four cars started the race but only 11 finished, as attrition took a heavy toll. *Chrysler Photographic Photo*

Fred Lorenzen's Ford lurches sideways as Tiny Lund takes quick evasive action in the 1966 National 500. Lorenzen had won the pole for the October event and was going for his fourth consecutive victory at Charlotte, having won the National 400 in 1964 and both events in 1965. He did not compete in the 1966 World 600 due to the Ford boycott. *CMS photo by Pal Parker*

LeeRoy Yarbrough whips his unsponsored No. 12 Dodge under Cale Yarborough in the 19th lap to take the lead in the 1966 National 500. Yarbrough started in 17th position, but it only took him 19 laps to grab first place. From that point on, he was only out of the lead for 15 laps when he made routine pit stops. Yarbrough thoroughly dominated the event and easily scored his first superspeedway victory. *CMS photo by Pal Parker*

of time falling inexorably through the hourglass, cool veteran Panch prevailed in the 4-hour, 26-minute marathon, winning by two laps over independent campaigner G. C. Spencer. Only 11 cars finished. Jarrett worked his way into second place but blew the engine in his Ford. Despite sitting out the final 32 laps, Jarrett still managed to land eighth in the final running order.

The Ford walkout ended in August, and for the first time since 1964, a full field of contenders was on hand at Charlotte Motor Speedway for the National 500. An extra 100 miles were added to the race, which attracted 66 entries for the 44-car field.

LeeRoy Yarbrough, driving a purple Dodge fielded by independent team owner Jon Thorne, whipped up on the favorites, leading for 311 of the 334 laps. It was Yarbrough's first big-track triumph.

As the curtain closed on Charlotte Motor Speedway's first six years, the facility had become one of the top attractions within the NASCAR-sanctioned boundaries—and its future was most promising.

CHAPTER 5

Musclecars and Mighty Men

1967–1970

Following two seasons of incessant squabbling among the automobile manufacturers and two costly boycotts precipitated by antiquated rules that were loosely interpreted and randomly enforced, the 1967 Grand National season appeared to hold the promise of an uninterrupted, intense campaign between Ford Motor Company and Chrysler Corporation.

Two-time series champion Ned Jarrett and the indomitable Marvin Panch retired following the 1966 season, and NASCAR's most illuminating star, Fred Lorenzen, suddenly hung up his helmet in April of 1967, creating a void that was quickly filled by a herd of hungry young chargers. Cale Yarborough, Buddy Baker, Bobby and Donnie Allison, Bobby Isaac, and LeeRoy Yarbrough were just a few of the youngsters eager to ventilate their lust for speed in top equipment and sprout into the upper echelon of the sport.

Richard Petty pits his Ford in the 1969 National 500. NASCAR's most prolific race winner drove a Ford during the 1969 season, winning nine times, including his 100th career victory at Winston-Salem, North Carolina. Petty started second in the 500-miler, but fell victim to an engine failure and did not finish. *CMS photo by Don Hunter*

Four-time Charlotte Motor Speedway winner Fred Lorenzen suddenly retired in April of 1967 at age 32. The Elmhurst, Illinois, driver racked up 26 NASCAR Grand National victories in less than six years and became one of stock car racing's brightest stars. For the 1967 World 600, Lorenzen was recruited by *The Charlotte News* to write a daily column for the evening newspaper. *CMS Archives*

Richard Petty (No. 43) and Bobby Allison (No. 6) battle door handle to door handle in the 1967 World 600. Allison finished third in the 600, which was his fifth effort with the Cotton Owens Dodge team. Petty ran fourth in the marathon event. Petty would win a record 27 Grand National events in 1967, a record still judged as unbeatable. *CMS Archives*

Dozens of teams engaged in extensive tire tests for Goodyear and Firestone in the weeks leading up to the eighth annual World 600. Manufacturers and tire companies placed tremendous emphasis on the Memorial Day weekend classic.

Cale Yarborough, who took the seat of the Wood Brothers Ford when Panch retired, won the pole with a four-lap average speed of 154.385 miles per hour. The stocky South Carolinian charged out of the starting blocks and led the first 24 laps, then surprisingly peeled into the pits for an unscheduled pit stop to replace badly blistered Firestone tires. Virtually all of the contenders followed suit, pitting early to replace shredded rubber.

Most of the front-runners who started on Firestones switched to Goodyears during the race, a practice fully legal under the 1967 NASCAR rules. Buddy Baker and his Ray Fox team stuck with the Firestones throughout the race and made 13 pit stops—an average of one pit stop every 30 miles. The two-car Petty Enterprises team changed 73 tires during the race.

Humpy Wheeler, then director of Firestone Racing, said the problem was the unexpected heat: "The track temperature was 131 degrees at noon and was up to 150 degrees after 100 miles. Rubber separates on the tires because the heat is so great. We were prepared for cars running 152 miles per hour on cooler surfaces. The cars started off at speeds of 154. We guessed wrong, that's all."

Jim Paschal, who qualified 10th in his Bill Ellis–prepared Plymouth, lumbered around on his Goodyears and found himself with a three-lap advantage on the field until he tagged the wall with 62 laps remaining. The 41-year-old veteran wrestled his ill-handling car the rest of the way, nosing out David Pearson and Bobby Allison at the finish for the victory.

Four days after the 600, president and general manager Richard Howard toted $296,000 to a bank

emerged from its darkest days to new heights of popularity.

During the summer of 1967, Richard Petty and his factory-backed Hemi-powered Plymouth GTX hit stride, winning Grand National races with staggering regularity. From June 6 through October 1, Petty won 19 of the 25 NASCAR Grand National races, including 10 straight—a record that will likely live in the record books forever.

Petty acquired the nickname "King Richard" during his winning streak, and he would be going for his 11th consecutive victory in Charlotte Motor Speedway's National 500. During Petty's record run, Ford Motor Company's top racing officials had become restless and bewildered at being unable to put a dent in the Petty express. For the 500, Ford had its guns fully loaded, bringing in a regiment of USAC stars with A. J. Foyt, Gordon Johncock, Mario Andretti, Whitey Gerkin, and Jack Bowsher seated in heavy artillery to join the regular Ford contingent. The Charlotte battle cry was "Stop Petty!"

Speedway general manager Richard Howard was instrumental in lifting the track from bankruptcy to profitability. Following the 1967 World 600, Howard paid off the final bank note and held a private mortgage-burning ceremony on the Speedway grounds. After seven years, the Speedway had finally escaped its dire financial straits. *CMS photo by T. Taylor Warren*

in Newton, North Carolina, clearing Charlotte Motor Speedway from all its debts. On Friday night, June 19, 1967, Howard initiated a "Mortgage Burning Ceremony" for speedway officials and invited guests. "Charlotte Motor Speedway is now free and clear of debts and we have money in the bank," Howard said proudly. Under the daring guidance of the tireless rotund, homespun dynamo, Charlotte Motor Speedway

LeeRoy Yarbrough was practicing in Junior Johnson's Ford in preparation for the 1967 National 500 when the fire extinguisher exploded inside the car while it was running at top speed. Blinded by the white fog, Yarbrough slid into the connection between a guard rail and a concrete wall, and the car practically disintegrated. The engine flew across the track, the front suspension ripped away, and the remains of the car came to a halt on the backstretch. Miraculously, Yarbrough escaped injury. He had to sit out the National 500 because in the 1960s teams were not permitted to bring in a back-up car that had not been previously entered. *CMS Archives*

The beefed-up Ford team suffered an embarrassment under the crystal blue Carolina skies as Chrysler products took eight of the first nine finishing positions. Dodge-driving Buddy Baker snapped Petty's winning streak with his first career Grand National victory. Only one factory-supported Ford finished the race, driven by third-place Dick Hutcherson. Petty was sidetracked when Andretti spun in the fourth turn, triggering a melee that took out three top Fords. Petty eventually retired with a blown engine.

Chrysler Corporation won 36 of the 49 NASCAR Grand National events in 1967 on the strength of a slender country boy from Level Cross, North Carolina. Richard Petty became the symbol of excellence for an entire sport populated by dozens of progressive, highly capable drivers. He engineered miracles every Sunday and thundered to his second NASCAR championship.

During the winter break between the 1967 and 1968 seasons, Ford Motor Company developed a sleek, aerodynamic Ford Torino and a Mercury with similar styling for the superspeedway wars. Plymouth

David Pearson skids through the third turn after getting sideswiped by Mario Andretti (No. 11) in the 1967 National 500. The incident precipitated a big crash, which took out several cars and ruined the hopes of many of the top contenders. *CMS photo by Pal Parker*

Buddy Baker pits his 1967 Dodge Charger during the 1967 National 500. Baker scored his first career victory at his hometown track, stopping Richard Petty's 10-race winning streak. Pit stops by the top teams frequently took upwards of 30 seconds in 1967. *Charlotte Motor Speedway*

had unveiled a new Roadrunner, and the Dodge bag of tricks included a new Charger model and an occasional Super Bee. The musclecar era had encroached on NASCAR in 1968, and their dynamic flair graced the high-banked speedways for the next three years.

In a complete turnaround from 1967, Ford dominated the early portion of the 1968 season, winning at Riverside, Daytona, Bristol, Richmond, Atlanta, North Wilkesboro, Martinsville, and Darlington. The new Ford models had their Chrysler rivals clearly covered. When the tour came to Charlotte for the ninth annual World 600, the Ford contingent was poised to continue its string of success in major events.

Damp weather and Dodge's Buddy Baker interrupted the Ford streak. Baker prevailed in a sloppy, soggy, rain-shortened affair that went only 382 1/2 miles. A total of 110 laps were run under the caution flag. At one time, 58 consecutive laps were run single-file behind the pace car while rain continued to fall. NASCAR officials took every step to avoid a one-week postponement. In 1968 there was no "next clear day" rule in the event of a rain-out.

Speedway offices and NASCAR headquarters were bombarded with complaints, both from the media and the paying spectators, about the way the 600 was handled. Rain began falling in the 98th lap and despite assurance that rain had set in for the day, NASCAR officials were determined to get the race past the halfway point. Had the 600 been postponed to the following week, two short-track events would have been canceled. One-hundred and fifty of the final 236 miles were run under the caution flag. Mercifully, the race was called off at 7 p.m. as more rain and darkness descended on the Speedway.

The developments in May had a direct relationship on an unprecedented decision in October when NASCAR's touring pros settled in for the National 500. Persistent rain began falling on Saturday and continued for more than 24 hours. When Sunday dawned, it was still raining and Speedway General Manager Richard Howard called the race off at 8 a.m. without consulting NASCAR officials.

"By golly, from now on at Charlotte Motor Speedway," Howard remarked sternly, "if it looks like they won't be able to race all the way, which is what people pay to see, we won't start the dad-blame thing."

With ill-feelings from May still lingering, NASCAR officials permitted Howard to postpone the National 500 until the following Sunday. Curiously, the weather cleared on its original scheduled date and the race could have been run in its entirety.

A disappointing crowd of only 35,000 dotted the grandstands a week later on Sunday, October 20. Remnants of Hurricane Gladys were raking the Carolina coast, and although the weather didn't affect the 500, it left its mark on the turnstiles.

The familiar Cotton Owens-owned No. 6 Dodge Charger was one of the sport's most formidable units in the 1960s. David Pearson and the car became champions in 1966. The 1967 season was not as productive. Six different drivers were seated in the Owens slope-backed car in 1967. Darel Dieringer drove the Owens Dodge in three races, including the 1967 National 500 at Charlotte Motor Speedway. *Dodge News Photo*

Charlie Glotzbach (No. 6) closes in on Richard Petty in the 1968 National 500. Glotzbach recorded his first NASCAR Grand National victory in the annual autumn classic and gave team owner Cotton Owens his first triumph on a superspeedway since 1960. *CMS photo by Pal Parker*

An exhausted LeeRoy Yarbrough and his wife, Gloria, share Victory Lane after winning the 1969 World 600. Yarbrough, a gifted and versatile speed artist, virtually rewrote the record books in 1969. He won seven superspeedway events, breaking the previous single-season record of four wins. Yarbrough won the Daytona 500 and the Firecracker 400 at Daytona, both races at Darlington, Charlotte's World 600, and 500-milers at Atlanta and Rockingham. *CMS photo by H. J. Rudes*

Sophomore Charlie Glotzbach, driving a Cotton Owens Dodge, whipped the field in a dazzling display of speed and nerve. It was the first career NASCAR victory for the Indiana driver, and the first for Dodge on a superspeedway since Baker won the 600 in May. At the close of the 1968 NASCAR season, Ford Motor Company had won 15 of the 20 major Grand National events.

In 1969 the introduction of the Ford Talladega and Mercury Spoiler models and the Blue Crescent 429-ci Boss engine enhanced Ford's domination. The Chrysler camp had made only peripheral refinements in its racing package. The outlook for the Mopar gang became bleak when Richard Petty jumped ship and signed a one-year contract to drive a Ford.

"It definitely looks like a better business opportunity with Ford," explained Petty, who had won 92 Grand National races with Plymouth. "We make our living by winning races. From what I've been able to observe, it looks like Ford is going to be better prepared to win in 1969. I want to get in on it."

The overall picture in NASCAR stock car racing was one of stupendous growth. New tracks were being built in Talladega, Texas, and Dover and Ontario, California. It was a lusty, demanding sport for a young, lusty, and demanding nation. At center stage was a collection of dynamic, goggled gladiators at the wheel of exotic American-made machinery.

Petty took his first ride in a Ford on Riverside's road course and promptly won the 500-miler. Despite not having the new engine approved in time for the Daytona 500, LeeRoy Yarbrough steered his Ford to victory in NASCAR's most celebrated event.

By the time the NASCAR tour came to Charlotte in May, Ford was undefeated on the superspeedways. Yarbrough, driving Junior Johnson's Mercury, whipped

The 10th annual National 500 was the second NASCAR event graced by the winged Dodge Daytona. James Hylton drove his No. 48 Daytona to an 11th place finish, while Richard Brickhouse's lime green No. 88 winged car bowed out early with engine problems. Curiously, Dr. Don Tarr's obsolete 1967 Charger finished ninth, his second consecutive top-10 finish on Charlotte's high banks. *CMS photo by Don Hunter*

Pole winner Bobby Isaac leads the field into the first turn just after the thundering start of the 1970 World 600. Cale Yarborough, David Pearson, Pete Hamilton, Fred Lorenzen (No. 28), and LeeRoy Yarbrough (No. 98) give close chase into the 24-degree banked corner. Lorenzen ended a three-year retirement and drove in the 600. He qualified sixth and was leading when the engine blew in his Dodge Daytona. *CMS Archives*

the star-studded field to win the 10th annual World 600. He led 274 of the 400 laps and finished two laps up on the field before a record trackside audience estimated at 75,000.

With a slim prospect of challenging the Fords on NASCAR's spiraling high banks, Chrysler's team of engineers, headed by Robert N. Rodger, unveiled plans to campaign a new, winged Dodge Daytona in the fall of 1969. "Aerodynamics is the next step left in the performance area," declared Rodger. "We've gone so far maximizing the use of engine power that we're looking elsewhere for improved performance, and there's a lot to do in aerodynamics. Ford built a Talladega and raced it at Daytona. We're going to build a Daytona and race it at Talladega."

Tests revealed the winged Dodge had an abundance of horsepower cloaked in an aerodynamic

shroud of complexities that allowed it to carve through the air with piercing quickness.

The inaugural Talladega 500, scheduled a month before Charlotte Motor Speedway's annual National 500, was marred by a massive drivers' boycott. NASCAR competitors formed the Professional Drivers Association in August and the strike at Talladega was an immediate action of their union. Speeds hovered near 200 miles per hour and tires were coming apart after just a few laps of practice. Virtually all the sport's top teams pulled their cars and drivers out of Talladega the day before the race. Only two Dodge Daytonas remained after the walkout. There were no factory-backed Fords in the event. Richard Brickhouse, a sophomore from the suburbs of Wilmington, North Carolina, won the Talladega 500 in his Ray Nichels–prepared Daytona.

Jim Vandiver (No. 31) chases James Hylton (No. 48) down the front chute during the 1970 World 600. Vandiver led six laps in the early going before having to go to the pits for extended mechanical repairs. When Vandiver returned to the track, he was 24 laps behind. Perseverance was rewarded, however, as he brought his Dodge Daytona home 10th. Had he not spent 24 laps in the pits, he would likely have finished second. *CMS Archives*

Charlotte Motor Speedway was host to the first full-fledged confrontation between the Ford Talladegas and the Dodge Daytonas. Cale Yarborough established a new track record with a 162.162 miles per hour lap in his Wood Brothers Mercury Spoiler, a mark that would stand for 11 years.

Donnie Allison prevailed in the 500 in his Banjo Matthews Ford, nipping the winged Dodges of Buddy Baker and Bobby Allison in a stretch duel. For the season, Ford Motor Company had dominated the big tracks, winning 14 of the 16 superspeedway events. Ford's accomplishments in 1968 and 1969 had been artistic successes but expensive ones.

During the 1970 Speedweeks in Daytona, Ford announced it would significantly reduce the factory support to its NASCAR teams. It was able to keep Richard Petty in its fold for only one season. Petty won nine races in Ford machinery in 1969, but only one had come on a superspeedway. He returned to Plymouth when Chrysler introduced the winged Super Bird. Pete Hamilton, a promising driver out of Dedham, Massachusetts, was tabbed to drive a Petty Super Bird in most of the big track events in 1970.

In one of the grand upsets in NASCAR history, Hamilton beat Ford's David Pearson in a memorable duel to capture the Daytona 500. All of the factory representatives from both Ford and Chrysler had been on hand at Daytona, but it wasn't until the 11th annual World 600 at Charlotte in May that all the industry-supported teams were again entered in a Grand National race.

Adding a little flavor to the 600 was live television coverage by ABC and the return of Fred Lorenzen after a three-year retirement. Speedway general manager Richard Howard, sensing Lorenzen's return would stimulate ticket sales, purchased for him a Dodge Daytona from team owner Mario Rossi and assembled a pit crew headed by Jack Sullivan, a mechanic with whom Lorenzen had worked in 1965 when both were members of the Holman-Moody Ford team.

"I told Freddy that if he wanted back, I'd help him," said Howard, who acknowledged spending about $20,000 in becoming a team owner for the 600. "I tried to get him a Ford, but each one I landed wasn't good enough for him. I finally bought the car from Rossi, and Chrysler naturally was happy to have him come back in a Dodge."

Jim Paschal, a two-time winner at Charlotte, also made a return. Having been fired by Chrysler after his productive 1967 season, the veteran driver had been out of the spotlight for over two years. In the World 600, he was seated in the familiar No. 43 Plymouth Super Bird in place of Richard Petty, who had suffered injuries in a nasty accident at Darlington two weeks earlier.

The 600 attracted nearly 80,000 spectators, many of them seated in the new double-decked Chrysler Tower grandstand near the fourth turn. Lorenzen and Paschal both ran with the leaders and led the race on occasion, but neither finished. Donnie Allison, with relief help from LeeRoy Yarbrough, took the lead late

Chargin' Charlie Glotzbach won the pole position for the 1970 National 500, which was the first restrictor plate race at Charlotte Motor Speedway. During the height of factory participation in NASCAR, Chrysler Corporation had catchy nicknames for its vibrant car colors. The purple Dodge Daytona driven by Glotzbach was nicknamed "Plum Crazy," although members of the print media jokingly referred to it as "Statutory Grape." *CMS Archives*

After recovering from successful bypass heart surgery, country-western singer Marty Robbins competed in the 1970 National 500, driving his lavender and yellow No. 42 Dodge Daytona. Robbins, who finished 12th in the 1967 National 500 in only his second career NASCAR Grand National start, departed with engine problems midway through the 1970 event. *CMS photo by Don Hunter*

in the race when David Pearson's Ford broke a transmission on pit road during his final routine stop. Eleven drivers swapped the lead 28 times in a highly competitive affair.

With speeds spiraling upwards at all the big tracks in 1970, restrictor plates were introduced by NASCAR in August. The restrictive devices were placed on all cars on all tracks, not just the ultra-fast ovals at Talladega and Daytona.

The final fling for the exotic musclecars at Charlotte Motor Speedway was the 11th annual National 500. The Chrysler wing cars dominated the proceedings, but LeeRoy Yarbrough parked his Junior Johnson Mercury in the winner's circle after Bobby Isaac's Dodge uncranked an engine in the waning laps. It would prove to be Yarbrough's final NASCAR Grand National triumph.

A week before the National 500, the racing world was saddened when news surfaced of the death of Curtis Turner, who perished when his private plane crashed in a remote area in Pennsylvania. Turner's life and career had been a passage in the fun house. He was handsome and high living, with an enormous talent for driving fast race cars and enjoying life.

Winds of change gusted freely with the close of the 1970 NASCAR season. R.J. Reynolds' Winston brand of cigarettes signed on to become title sponsor of the series effective in 1971, and the automotive factories sharply cut their support from American motorsports. Ford withdrew its support entirely, and Chrysler's industry-supported camp was reduced to a two-car team fielded out of the Petty Enterprises shops. The special-edition, racing-oriented models like the Ford Talladega and the Chrysler winged warriors were all but legislated out of business with deeper engine restrictions.

With the advent of restrictor plates and the demise of the American musclecar on public highways, a crisp, colorful, and indispensable chapter in NASCAR stock car racing had come to an end.

LeeRoy Yarbrough and crew chief Herb Nab savor the rewards of victory after the 1970 National 500. For Yarbrough, it was his 13th and final NASCAR Grand National victory—and his third victory at Charlotte Motor Speedway. With the factory retreat, Yarbrough was unable to land a full-time ride and disappeared from the tour in late 1972. *CMS Archives*

CHAPTER 6

Stumbling into the Modern Era

1971–1974

America's musclecars and the high-octane hybrids of Ford and Chrysler had performed splendidly on NASCAR's center stage in the late 1960s and 1970. In 1971 they were replaced by more conventional offerings from Detroit and Dearborn.

R.J. Reynolds came on board to sponsor the NASCAR Winston Cup Grand National tour, a coup for the entire sport that had long-range benefits. The immediate consequence, however, was a lack of sponsorship dollars for the race teams. Cale Yarborough departed NASCAR to join the USAC Indy Car series, stepping out of the highly regarded Wood Brothers Mercury. During the course of the season, several team owners either quit entirely or substantially cut back their efforts due to tight finances. Junior Johnson and Banjo Matthews, two of Ford's top team owners, pulled off the tour shortly after the Daytona 500.

A. J. Foyt, racing icon with unsurpassed versatility, competed in seven NASCAR Winston Cup Grand National races in 1971. He won two of the races and was the fastest qualifier five times. The fiery Texan drove a Banjo Matthews–groomed Chevrolet (No. 27) in the 1971 National 500 at Charlotte. Steering problems forced him out midway through the race. *CMS Archives*

For the first time in several years, a white No. 3 Chevrolet hit the high banks of Charlotte Motor Speedway. In an effort to stimulate ticket sales during a depressionary state of stock car racing in 1971, Speedway president Richard Howard funded the team managed by colorful and cantankerous Junior Johnson. The legendary Johnson drove a Chevrolet to seven victories in 1963, including Charlotte's National 400. Hard-charging Charlie Glotzbach took the controls of the Monte Carlo, winning the pole for the 1971 World 600. *CMS Archives*

Trackside attendance began another downward spiral, and although R.J. Reynolds' involvement represented stability in the sport, competition on the speedways was declining. That all changed when the tour came to Charlotte Motor Speedway for the 12th annual World 600.

Speedway general manager Richard Howard spoke with Junior Johnson about the possibility of returning in a Chevrolet. On April 8, 1971, Howard made an announcement. "I have made a deal with Junior to build the Chevy. And it could be the most competitive Chevy to race since General Motors quit backing stock car racing in 1963. I wish Junior would drive it, but if he won't, we'll have a good man behind the wheel," said Howard, who was officially listed in NASCAR records as team owner of the new operation.

The 39-year-old Johnson declined to drive the Chevrolet Monte Carlo in the World 600, so Charlie Glotzbach, one of many drivers to lose his ride when the factories retreated, was tabbed to drive the white #3 Chevy, painted identically to the car Johnson drove to victory at Charlotte in 1963.

In qualifying, Glotzbach promptly went out and won the pole position, and—not surprisingly—a record crowd turned out on a cool, overcast afternoon to watch the race. Glotzbach led the 600 on four occa-

sions for 78 laps but crashed into the front stretch wall on lap 234 while running second. Within moments of the crash, Howard made an appearance in the speedway press box. Track publicist Bob Latford introduced Howard, saying, "And now, we'll have a word from the car owner."

Howard took the microphone and told the members of the media, "I just want to let everyone know that we're real happy with the way the car ran today, and we're going to build another one for the National 500 in October."

Bobby Allison, new chauffeur for the Holman-Moody team, won the 600, with brother Donnie Allison second in the Wood Brothers Mercury.

The Howard-Johnson Chevrolet was rebuilt well before October and competed sparingly during the summer of 1971, showing up when and where track promoters were willing to pay a handsome appearance fee. Glotzbach wheeled the car to victory at Bristol, Chevrolet's first win in a major NASCAR race since 1963.

Joining Glotzbach in highly regarded Chevrolets for the National 500 were LeeRoy Yarbrough and A. J. Foyt. Yarbrough was at the controls of a team Chevrolet built by Johnson, while Foyt was in a Banjo Matthews Monte Carlo partially funded by Richard Howard.

Bobby Allison left his own independent Dodge operation in the spring of 1971 and joined the Holman-Moody Mercury team. The undisputed leader of the Alabama Gang won 10 events from May through November, including both events at Charlotte. Allison enjoys the Victory Lane ceremonies with his wife, Judy, and Miss Coca-Cola, Sharon Brown, following the 1971 National 500. *CMS Archives*

Yarbrough and Foyt failed to go the distance and Glotzbach finished fifth. Bobby Allison won the rain-interrupted event for his second straight win at Charlotte Motor Speedway. Crowd estimates were in the 52,000 range, held back by heavy weekend rains, a delayed start, and unseasonably cool temperatures.

By 1972, the NASCAR Winston Cup Grand National series was reduced to 31 events, all covering 250 miles or more. The 100- and 150-milers, a staple of NASCAR's flagship series since its inception in 1949, were gone, tossed into a short-lived Grand National East division, which did not survive past 1973.

Bobby Allison left the Holman-Moody Mercury team at the end of 1971 and joined the Howard-Johnson unit, bringing the Coca-Cola sponsorship with him. Allison emerged as an immediate title contender, battling Richard Petty for the annual chase for the championship. Through the first 10 races of the 1972 slate, Allison and Petty collectively won six times.

Following the 500-lapper at Martinsville in April, Allison discovered that he would have an unlikely teammate for the 13th annual World 600: Wendell Scott, a 50-year-old black campaigner out of Danville, Virginia, who was struggling mightily with his equipment. He had made the field—and created an indelible impression—at Martinsville, the first race he qualified for all year.

"I worked all week building an engine for my old Ford," said Scott. "It blew when I was taking it off the tow truck. I went back home, removed the 1966 street engine from my son's car, and put it in my racer. That's what I ran the race with." Scott finished 16th in the field, 44 laps behind winner Richard Petty. During one pit stop, he climbed out of his car to help his ragtag crew change tires.

Richard Howard was on hand at Martinsville and had observed Scott's trials and tribulations. "I feel sorry for Wendell," Howard said. "I took a look at his old car and realized how much trouble he's had. He's never had a chance. Well, I decided to give him a Chevrolet for the World 600."

Scott was emotionally grateful for Howard's goodwill gesture. "I don't know what to say except that I appreciate it so much," said Scott. "That race car will seem like a Cadillac to me." Scott qualified 11th on the first day of World 600 time trials at 152.810 miles per hour. Allison earned the pole with a 158.162 miles per hour. Allison dominated the race, leading 239 laps before a cut tire forced him to make an unscheduled pit stop in the closing laps. He finished second to Buddy Baker's Dodge.

Scott's much-heralded ride turned into a dud. He was lapped after just 36 miles. The veteran managed to

The General Motors contingent was well represented in the 1971 National 500 with LeeRoy Yarbrough (No. 98), A. J. Foyt (No. 27), and Charlie Glotzbach (No. 3). Glotzbach won the pole and finished fifth in the rain-shortened 500-miler. Yarbrough and Foyt failed to finish. *CMS Archives*

Journeyman campaigner Wendell Scott participated in the Victory Lane ceremonies following the 1972 World 600. The veteran from Danville, Virginia, drove a Chevrolet owned by Charlotte Motor Speedway president Richard Howard and built by Junior Johnson. While he failed to finish the race, Scott was the recipient of the inaugural Curtis Turner Memorial Award for Outstanding Achievement. With Scott are Turner's widow, Bunny, and Union 76 RaceStopper Royette Tarry. *CMS photo by Suther Studio*

climb into the top 10, but his engine blew after 283 laps. Scott, the only African-American driver to win an official NASCAR Winston Cup race, wound up 22nd in the final rundown.

The latter part of the 1972 season was strictly a Petty-Allison affair, sprinkled with a liberal amount of fender rubbing and a high-octane mixture of fussin' and cussin'. Petty prevailed in a devouring slugfest at North Wilkesboro a week before the National 500. It was the fourth time in the previous six races that Petty and Allison had finished in the top two spots.

Allison and Petty forged to the front in the National 500 with Allison having matters well in hand until Petty spun and crashed with 16 laps remaining. Petty's mishap set the stage for an electrifying duel between Allison and Buddy Baker, who had recently taken the controls of the K&K Insurance Dodge when Bobby Isaac suddenly stepped out of the ride.

The lead changed hands five times over the last nine laps as the crowd of 73,000 cheered wildly. Allison dashed across the finish line first, beating Baker in a near photo-finish. David Pearson and A. J. Foyt were third and fourth, respectively, in a pair of Mercurys fielded by the Wood Brothers.

By 1973, Cale Yarborough was back in the NASCAR fold after two unproductive seasons in USAC Indy Cars. Yarborough took the wheel of Junior Johnson's Chevrolet when Allison decided to field his own team.

David Pearson, who stepped into the Wood Brothers Mercury in 1972, hit stride and was virtually unstoppable in 1973. Entering the World 600, Pearson was riding a personal five-race winning streak, having won every race in which he finished.

Spicing up the 600 was Richard Howard's brainchild, the "Big Chance Special." A new Chevrolet Laguna prepared by Junior Johnson was open to the driver who garnered the most votes in a nationwide campaign. Over one million votes were cast and Late Model Sportsman campaigner Billy Scott of Union, South Carolina, received more than 72,000 votes. During open house festivities a week before the 600, Scott crashed the new car out of turn four. It was hastily rebuilt, but Scott was rendered to mid-pack during the 13th annual running of NASCAR's longest and most punishing event.

Buddy Baker beat Pearson in a sizzling duel before an audience of 85,000 for his fourth triumph on the Charlotte mile-and-a-half. An interested observer was one Olin Bruton Smith, who was making his first appearance at Charlotte Motor Speedway in over a decade. Smith had been purchasing large chunks of stock and had compiled enough to be one of the most powerful board members. Smith was instrumental in scheduling a 300-mile NASCAR Late Model Sportsman race the day before the 14th annual National 500. Sponsored by World Service Life Insurance Company in Fort Worth, Texas, the 300-miler quickly established itself as one of the premier autumn events for what is now regarded as the NASCAR Busch Series.

Bobby Allison won the 300-miler on Saturday, October 6, 1973. But other news at Charlotte Motor Speedway that day grabbed more headlines than Allison's victory. Charlie Glotzbach had put his Hoss Ellington Chevrolet on the pole for the National 500 during a qualifying run on Wednesday before the race. His pole-winning effort was disallowed on Saturday morning, however, when NASCAR inspectors found an illegal trick carburetor plate in Glotzbach's car.

The NASCAR-mandated carburetor plate was rigged with a cable running from the plate to the driver's compartment. Conveniently, Glotzbach could tug on the cable and remove the restrictor plate during the race. Glotzbach admitted the illegal device was in the car for Saturday's practice session. "We got caught. But we didn't qualify with the cheater plate on. We put it in on Saturday to do a little experimenting. From the looks of the goings-on in the garage area, that's what it's going to take to win or even lead the race," said Glotzbach.

A popular theory during the fall of 1973 was that several teams discovered methods of getting around the

Buddy Baker and crew chief Richie Barsz share a pensive moment in Victory Lane after the 1972 World 600. Driving a Petty Enterprises Dodge, Baker scored his third triumph at the Speedway. Later in the 1972 season, he departed the Petty team and took a seat in Nord Krauskopf's K&K Insurance Dodge. *CMS Archives*

Entering the 1973 World 600, David Pearson and the Wood Brothers Mercury No. 21 were on a five-race winning streak, not having lost a race since the Daytona 500. Buddy Baker, wheeling the Harry Hyde–wrenched No. 71 Dodge, was seeking his first win of the season. Baker prevailed in a tense late-race duel and ended Pearson's winning streak. It was a flash of déjà vu for Baker, who stopped Richard Petty's 10-race winning streak with a victory at Charlotte in 1967. *CMS Archives*

Bobby Allison pits his Chevrolet during the 1973 National 500, which turned out to be one of the most controversial races in Charlotte Speedway history. Allison finished third behind Cale Yarborough and Richard Petty, but filed a protest immediately following the event. NASCAR officials examined the engines in the first- and second-place cars, and the exact findings remain a mystery today. *Greg Fielden*

carburetor restrictor plates, which were in place at all Winston Cup Grand National events. For the National 500, lap leader awards of $34,400—$100 to the leader of each lap—served as an incentive too tempting for some teams to resist.

Journalist Benny Phillips remarked, "The penalty of disqualifying Glotzbach is like putting someone in jail on Saturday for getting drunk on Wednesday." In an unprecedented ruling by NASCAR after collaboration with Richard Howard, Glotzbach was permitted to requalify late Saturday afternoon and start the National 500 36th on the grid. Howard wanted and needed Glotzbach in the 500 field. The unusual ruling remains the only time on record that NASCAR has permitted a

car to requalify after time trials had ended. Details on why the decision was made remain a mystery today.

Glotzbach charged from 36th to lead the National 500 by the 32nd lap. But he was involved in a heavy crash with David Pearson in the 46th lap, eliminating both along with rookie sensation Darrell Waltrip. Cale Yarborough and Richard Petty ran away from the field, leading for 310 of the 334 laps collectively. Yarborough beat Petty by 1.4 seconds and Bobby Allison finished third, three full laps behind.

After the race, NASCAR officials conducted an official post-race inspection, which lasted until 10:15 p.m. The findings were sent to NASCAR headquarters in Daytona Beach for further ruling.

The way the controversy was handled struck a nerve with Richard Howard, general manager of Charlotte Motor Speedway and official owner of the car Yarborough had apparently driven to victory. "NASCAR can give you a stamp of approval at race time and six hours later can't give you a winner. I've been paying NASCAR inspectors to be here all week and ensure that the cars are legal. Now they tell me they might not have done their job and some illegal cars may have gotten by them. If so, what have I been spending my money for?"

The official results didn't come from NASCAR until Monday evening at 5 p.m. NASCAR's announcement said the results would stand, with Yarborough and Petty finishing first and second, because the unnamed violations were "borderline." NASCAR cited "inadequacies" in the inspection procedure.

"The decision was made following a meeting of NASCAR officials after reviewing information in a post-race inspection. The procedure used to check all of the engine sizes in the pre-race inspection proved inadequate," said the statement released from the Daytona Beach headquarters.

Yarborough got to keep the $45,425 first prize in the most controversial race of the 1973 NASCAR season.

In the autumn of 1973, the very survival of NASCAR racing was being threatened, but not from the lingering residue of the National 500 fiasco. This was much more serious—a gripping energy and fuel shortage that stretched to all points of the globe. NASCAR and other forms of professional racing cleared the early season obstacles, and the length of all Winston Cup Grand National races was reduced by 10 percent.

Although NASCAR hoped to phase out the big-block engines and their encumbering restrictor plates as early as 1971, they stayed in use, because teams were finding the change to small blocks terribly expensive. In 1974, however, in an accelerated effort to remove the restrictor plates, NASCAR rules were altered regularly during the early part of the season.

At the age of 23, Dale Earnhardt competed in his first race at Charlotte Motor Speedway. Driving a Dodge arranged by Speedway President Richard Howard, and entered by veteran driver Neil Castles, Earnhardt started 12th and finished 13th in the 1974 World Service Life 300 NASCAR Late Model Sportsman event. *CMS Archives*

Bobby Allison noses his No. 12 Chevrolet just ahead of challengers L. D. Ottinger (No. 2) and Jack Ingram in the stunning finish to the second-annual World Service Life 300 for NASCAR Late Model Sportsman cars. The lead changed hands 23 times among nine drivers in one of the most competitive events ever staged at the Speedway. *CMS Archives*

Teams unwilling to make the switch from big to small engines suffered from heavier restrictive devices. The smallblock engine, limited to 355 ci, was the way to go. For the remainder of the 1974 NASCAR season, races were conducted with some cars running with restrictor plates and others competing with free-breathing smallblocks.

At Charlotte Motor Speedway, Bruton Smith had been voted chairman of the board of directors and began sharing expansion ideas and methods of implementing vast improvements. A new 5,000-seat Grand National Tower grandstand located near the entrance to turn one was in place by May of 1974.

The 15th annual World 600 was a 540-mile affair. The first 40 laps were not scored and the green flag signaled the beginning of the 41st lap. David Pearson, Richard Petty, and Cale Yarborough treated the crowd of 84,000 to a tremendous duel. Pearson snared the lead with nine laps remaining and nosed out Petty by 0.6 seconds. Yarborough was knocked out 18 laps from the finish when he slid in a patch of oil and clobbered the retaining wall. It was Pearson's 80th career NASCAR Winston Cup Grand National win and his first at Charlotte Motor Speedway since 1961.

While holding a position of authority, Smith proved quite generous in pouring money back into the facility. A 2.25-mile road course was built in the infield and a new section of grandstands was erected at the first turn. The Charlotte Motor Speedway was host to an International Motor Sports Association (IMSA) event in August of 1974. Peter Gregg drove a Porsche to victory in the 300-mile Grand Touring event. Five NASCAR drivers—Buddy Baker, David Pearson, Cale Yarborough, Bobby Isaac, and Elmo Langley—were recruited and competed as well. Baker, teaming with veteran road racer Gene Felton, took home fourth-place money.

A rock concert was also on the Charlotte Motor Speedway agenda in August, which drew an audience

of 200,000 fans who reveled in the amplified noise for two days.

Bobby Allison won the second annual World Service Life 300 NASCAR Late Model Sportsman race. The event was perhaps one of the best events in Speedway history as Allison, Jack Ingram, and L. D. Ottinger crossed the finish line three abreast.

The 10 percent reduction in race distance for the Winston Cup Grand National series was waived by NASCAR in July. The 15th annual National 500 attracted nearly 60 entries in the next-to-last race on the 1974 schedule. During initial practice runs, Buddy Baker was consistently quickest in Bud Moore's Ford. In Wednesday qualifying, however, Baker lost control on his second lap and spun through the fourth turn, flatspotting the tires. His first lap of time trials secured the third starting position.

Moore wanted to place two new right-side tires on Baker's Ford for the race, but the request was turned down by NASCAR technical director Bill Gazaway. In a fit of anger, Moore took a pocket knife and slashed the two right-side tires flat.

Gazaway was not amused. "Each team may change one tire on each side, but a second one could force them to start at the rear of the field. But I know why they're flat, and we'll take that into consideration," Gazaway said.

On Friday morning, NASCAR officials declared that Baker would have to start at the rear of the field. An optimistic minority of one, Baker promised a relentless charge to the front on Sunday. "I'll be 10th in two laps . . . or I'll be wiped out," the driver said.

Baker, going for his fifth win at Charlotte Motor Speedway, charged past 10 cars in the opening lap. As he was completing his second lap, a massive 10-car crash occurred along the home chute. Rookie Jerry Schild wiggled off turn four, corrected his errant machine, and darted across the infield grass. Schild's car kicked up a cloud of dust, which momentarily obscured the view of trailing drivers. Baker collided with Dick Brooks, triggering the melee.

Two cars slashed through the inside guard rail, seven cars were completely destroyed, and Marty Robbins was sent to Charlotte Memorial Hospital with facial lacerations. The caution flag was out for nearly a half-hour as crews made repairs to the retaining barrier.

A total of 47 lead changes kept the estimated crowd of 56,000 on their collective feet most of the afternoon and David Pearson edged Richard Petty in a close finish to post his second straight victory at Charlotte.

NASCAR Winston Cup Grand National racing stumbled into the Modern Era on shaky ground with the loss of factory support and several of its top drivers, but by the end of 1974 the sport had stabilized remarkably.

CHAPTER 7

Speeding Into New Frontiers

1975–1977

The 1975 NASCAR Winston Cup Grand National season represented a coming of age for the sport of stock car racing. The energy crisis of 1974, which threatened the very existence of auto racing, subsided and oil was once again plentiful in America, albeit much more expensive. The constant bickering about mandated restrictor plates with varying degrees of horsepower-choking devices died down as well. All teams completed the costly and lengthy transition from fuel-gulping big engines to smaller power plants.

In addition to the stabilized technical guidelines, NASCAR racing had other promising ventures on the horizon. Television contracts were becoming more plentiful and the rewards were greater. ABC Sports paid close to $300,000 for television rights for the Daytona 500, the final 90 minutes of which was aired live. Ratings were impressive as Benny Parsons' unlikely Daytona 500 triumph grabbed a 10.7 rating, comfortably winning its time slot against CBS's NBA basketball game (8.6) and NBC's NHL hockey game (4.1).

Forty-two thoroughbred NASCAR Winston Cup cars made up the field for the 1975 World 600 at Charlotte Motor Speedway. Driving Ed Negre's blue-and-yellow No. 8 Dodge Charger was 24-year-old Dale Earnhardt, making his first start in big-league competition. Earnhardt earned the 33rd starting spot with a qualifying speed of 151.290 miles per hour. The second-generation driver finished 22nd. *CMS Archives*

NASCAR's stunning success in the Nielsen ratings lit the burners to the boosters of this suddenly rocketing sport. Record crowds turned out to watch what happened when the best stock car drivers and finely tuned vehicles fearlessly made the speed-laced 500-mile sojourn on America's high-banked speedways. Although a number of early season events had less than capacity starting fields, the popularity within the NASCAR boundaries was exploding.

Expansion and upgrading of the nation's racing facilities became an instant priority, from the hamlets that suckled most of the short tracks to the vast superspeedways, most of which were within a short drive from major markets. Charlotte Motor Speedway became the unquestioned leader in this expansion.

Energetic Richard Howard served his final year as president of the Charlotte Motor Speedway in 1975, having prevailed by a narrow four-to-three vote in a board meeting election on March 4, 1975, and he retained his post-presidency. Co-founder Bruton Smith continued to serve as chairman of the board. While Howard and Smith did not see eye to eye on several key matters concerning the growth

Crusty veteran Jack Ingram was a staple in the NASCAR Late Model Sportsman and Busch Series for nearly four decades. Affectionately nicknamed "The Iron Man," Ingram won five national championships, including a trifecta in 1972, 1973, and 1974. His familiar burgundy No. 11 Chevrolet was a fixture at Charlotte, competing in 31 Saturday events. Twice he finished second in the 300-miler. *CMS Archives*

David Pearson (No. 21) leads a slightly cocked Cale Yarborough (No. 11) and Richard Childress (No. 96) during the 1975 World 600. While Yarborough won three races in 1975, he and his Junior Johnson team suffered through a character-building season sprinkled with 14 DNFs in his 27 starts. *CMS Archives*

and expansion of the facility, extensive track improvements continued rapidly.

Richard Petty, five-time champion of the NASCAR kingdom, won five of the first dozen races in 1975. Entering the 16th edition of the World 600, Petty had a sizable lead in the points and he was going for his first major victory at Charlotte Motor Speedway. Petty had, however, scored an official NASCAR victory in a 100-mile qualifying race at Charlotte in 1961. "That was the only year they ran the qualifiers," said Petty before the World 600, "and most people forgot about that since it really wasn't any more than a heat race. From my standpoint, I still haven't won a big race at Charlotte."

Olin Bruton Smith always had lofty visions. The Oakboro, N.C., native possesses the energy to overcome seemingly impossible odds and carry his visions from ideas to reality. A co-founder of Charlotte Motor Speedway, Smith returned in the mid-1970s and began an ambitious expansion of the speedway grounds. Providing the spectators with state-of-the-art facilities, Smith has been a major force in the explosive growth of NASCAR Winston Cup racing. *CMS Archives*

Petty was besieged by the record number of media representatives before the 600. "I have to look at the World 600 as just another race, except that it pays more than most," he said before qualifying time trials. "If I worried about not winning at Charlotte, I'd really have myself psyched out by now.

"I do feel I have just as good a chance to win as anybody else right now, but I'm not going to be overly optimistic or pessimistic. I remember when I had the record streak going [in 1967], and that all ended when I wrecked. The first thing I hear from the press when I show up in the speedway garage is a reminder of the jinx. But I try not to think about it. One of these days some freak thing is going to happen and the cat who drives the number 43 is going to win one here."

Petty's quest for the prize that managed to sidestep his craftsmanship for 15 years kept him in the headlines all week. He qualified third behind perennial pole sitter David Pearson and a surprising effort by independent Lennie Pond, who bumped Petty off the front row in a late run against the clock.

As race time grew near, the pressure mounted on Petty to conquer the Charlotte mile-and-a-half. "If you can't win the Daytona 500, you want to win the 600," said Petty. "For prestige-wise and recognition-wise, the 600 is the second-most important race of the year. It's a must for every team that didn't win Daytona."

The field of 40 was determined in three days of qualifying. Joining Petty in the diverse World 600 field was 24-year-old youngster Dale Earnhardt, who was making his first NASCAR Winston Cup Grand National start in a Dodge fielded by journeyman campaigner Ed Negre. Also in the field was Tennessean Randy Bethea, the first African-American to compete in the big leagues since Wendell Scott's retirement in 1973.

The 600 got under way beneath clear skies, with temperatures pushing 90 degrees. A record crowd of 90,600 was on hand in the sweltering weather. Petty dropped back at the start, hampered by what he called "severe handling problems." He pitted twice in the first 54 laps and fell two laps off the pace. With the help of chassis adjustments and a series of timely caution flags,

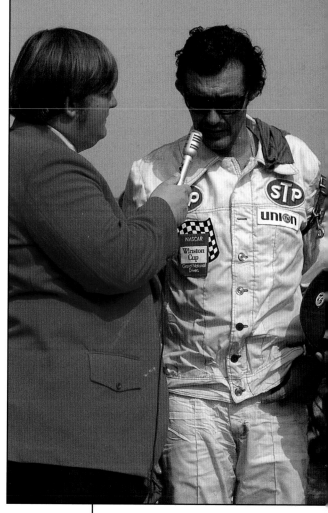

Public address announcer Bill Connell interviews Richard Petty in Victory Lane following The King's victory in the 1975 World 600. The triumph was the 170th of Petty's illustrious career but his first in a long-distance event at Charlotte Motor Speedway. *CMS Archives*

H. A. "Humpy" Wheeler kicked around the Carolina dirt tracks during his adolescence and learned the tricks of the promotional trade. By 1976 he had become president and general manager of the Speedway. He is largely recognized as the master showman in motorsports and has become one of the most powerful executives in NASCAR. *CMS Archives*

Petty scrambled back into contention after 250 miles. Once he grabbed command in the 166th lap, Petty sped away from his rivals and crossed the finish line a full lap ahead of runner-up Cale Yarborough.

Earnhardt wound up in 22nd place, completing 355 of the 400 laps. Bethea lost an engine in his Chevrolet near the 400-mile mark and wound up 33rd.

"I think this win means more to the crew than to me," Petty said, deflecting the adulation to his Petty Enterprises crew led by Dale Inman and brother Maurice Petty. "We've achieved a lot here this week. We've now won a 600, but I haven't won a 500."

By the time the touring pros returned to Charlotte in October for the 16th edition of the National 500, Petty had won 11 races and was virtually assured of his sixth Winston Cup title.

A crowd of 21,000 turned out to watch Wednesday's qualifying session. David Pearson snatched the pole and a record $10,400 prize with a speed of 161.701 miles per hour. Dave Marcis's K&K Insurance Dodge was a distant second, nearly 2 miles per hour off Pearson's pace. "Pearson was running like he stole something," barked Marcis. Petty qualified ninth in the field of 42. A. J. Foyt and outspoken youngster Darrell Waltrip filled the second row.

Ray Hendrick, 46-year-old grandfather from Virginia, captured the third annual World Service Life 300 for NASCAR Late Model Sportsman cars, nipping newcomer Neil Bonnett in a stretch duel. Hendrick collected $20,300 from a record purse of $100,000, the richest Late Model Sportsman race in NASCAR history.

Petty kept the leaders in sight during the early laps of the 500, then applied the spurs to his STP steed and led the final 166 miles to score his second-straight Charlotte victory. Petty kept Pearson at bay in the final stretch, winning by two car lengths.

"I feel like a coach whose team was pushed all over the field but got beat by only a point or two," said Pearson. "It wasn't that close. He was toying with me."

A developing shift of direction for Charlotte Motor Speedway became official on Thursday morning, January 29, 1976, when Richard Howard resigned as president and general manager. Bruton Smith appointed Howard Augustus "Humpy" Wheeler, Jr., as new president to implement his progressive ideas. Smith, deeply interested in the formation of a showcase cathedral complete with all the trimmings, was anxious for his ideas to succeed. Wheeler, who had been groomed for his role in 1975 when he was appointed director of development, had the natural aptitude of the Smith system. Smith's visions were enhanced by the competence of the men in his command.

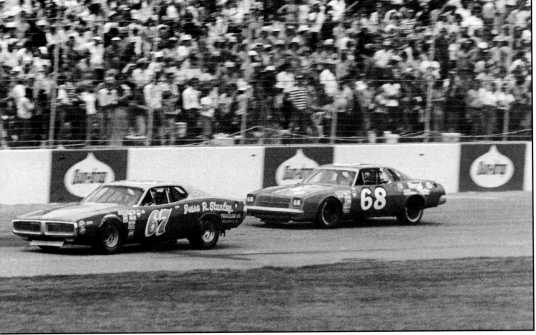

Janet Guthrie, a veteran of sports car road racing, rocked the motorsports world in 1976 by announcing her intentions of competing in the Indianapolis 500. While her efforts to secure a spot in the 33-car field failed, she did land a seat in the No. 68 Chevrolet for the 17th annual World 600, becoming the first female to drive in a Winston Cup event at Charlotte. Guthrie turned in an admirable effort in the 600, finishing 15th. Buddy Arrington (No. 67) finished just ahead of Guthrie in 14th place. *CMS Archives*

"Bruton has a great reputation for making money and he has a great understanding of how you make a place look first-class," Wheeler asserted. "He has some lofty ideas."

Not only did Wheeler take the reins of Charlotte Motor Speedway, he became the nonpareil promoter for NASCAR stock car racing. "Intense competition is commonplace in Winston Cup racing," he said. "It is this quality of racing that will make 1976 the biggest year in NASCAR history. Over the years the public, which only buys that which is constantly good, had judged Winston Cup racing to be the most competitive in the world. And with the improving economy, they can now patronize the sport that is giving them consistently good entertainment.

"The volume of ticket requests is so great that our ticket office has now started operating on Sunday. We are entering a new era in Winston Cup racing. The saying used to be racing is the sport of the seventies, but now it should be Winston Cup racing is the sport of the seventies," said Wheeler.

The sport of the seventies received a promotional shot in the arm when Janet Guthrie, a 38-year-old Florida-born physicist living in New York, attempted but failed to earn a starting spot in the 60th running of the

Dale Earnhardt, who cut his teeth on the short tracks around the Carolinas, was an instant marvel behind the wheel of a NASCAR Winston Cup race car. He could race three-abreast in congested corners without flinching. Three times he drove a short-track Nova in the Late Model Sportsman races at Charlotte. Despite the car's disadvantages on a superspeedway, he finished 6th in 1975, 14th in 1976, and 5th in 1977. *CMS Archives*

David Pearson drove the Wood Brothers Mercury to victory in the 1976 World 600. The triumph represented a sparkling link in a golden chain of near-perfection during the 1976 NASCAR Winston Cup campaign. Pearson won 10 of 22 starts in 1976 and started on the front row 12 times. *CMS Archives*

Harry Gant acquired the handle "Mr. October" with his fantastic winning skein in 1991, but Virginia's Ray Hendrick compiled an envious record during the October Late Model Sportsman events at Charlotte Motor Speedway. Hendrick competed in six October events on the mile-and-a-half, won twice, and registered three fourth-place efforts and one ninth-place finish. *CMS Archives*

Indianapolis 500. Unable to make the 33-car grid at Indy, Guthrie flew on a private aircraft supplied by Bruton Smith into Charlotte, where arrangements were hastily made to get her a car for the 17th annual World 600.

Guthrie's experience was in road racing, and she had never seen a stock car race. Lynda Ferreri, a 32-year-old executive at First Union National Bank in Charlotte, became an instant "NASCAR team owner," having purchased a Hoss Ellington Chevrolet that A. J. Foyt had driven in the Daytona 500. "About a week ago, when Janet was trying to qualify for the Indianapolis 500, a friend of mine said, 'She's a hoax,' " Ferreri explained. "Well, I didn't like that and I got on the phone to see what I'd have to do to put her in this race [World 600]. The (Charlotte Motor) Speedway is not behind it. I am personally responsible for it. I bought the car."

Guthrie qualified for the 600, earning the 27th starting slot with a speed of 157.797 miles per hour. David Pearson won the pole at 159.132 miles per hour.

On Friday, J. V. Reins captured the 200-km event for NASCAR's Baby Grand Series, an event in which Lillian Vandiver, sister of Winston Cup's Jim Vandiver, became the first female competitor in an oval race at Charlotte Motor Speedway. A broken fan belt relegated Vandiver to a 29th place finish.

The Patriot 300 for NASCAR Modified cars was slated for Saturday. Heavy rains interrupted the open-wheel event, and Darrell Waltrip was declared the winner at 8:49 p.m. after 198 miles had been completed.

Skies cleared for the World 600 and a record announced crowd of 103,000 turned out to watch a slice of history. All reserved seats were sold out by 10:30 a.m. on Sunday, and 20 minutes later the infield was shut off to vehicular traffic.

The lead swapped hands 38 times with David Pearson leading 16 times for 230 laps. He edged Richard Petty for his fourth victory at Charlotte. Guthrie drove a conservative race, finishing 15th, 21 laps behind the winner.

After completing the 4-hour, 22-minute marathon, Guthrie was presented six roses by her pit crew headed by Ralph Moody and Will Cronkrite. "It was my most taxing race physically," she remarked, "but it was an absolutely fantastic experience. I think I drove a fairly clean race. With more experience, I think I'll be better able to handle heavy traffic."

Pearson was enjoying a magnificent season in 1976, winning nine of his 18 starts when the NASCAR tour checked into Charlotte Motor Speedway for the 17th National 500. Humpy Wheeler devised a "Stop Pearson Movement" and recruited

several top-rank USAC drivers to participate in the $216,555 chase.

"I haven't got a thing against David, or Glen and Leonard Wood," said Wheeler, "but I think it would be good for the sport and arouse more interest from fans if somebody else won a big race for a change."

During Wheeler's promotional campaign, title-bound Cale Yarborough began a winning streak of his own, racking up four straight Winston Cup victories in a 22-day period. Joining Pearson and Yarborough as headliners were Indy 500 champions A. J. Foyt, Gordon Johncock, and Johnny Rutherford, and road racer

Al Holbert, along with the regular contingent of NASCAR regulars.

Pearson bagged his seventh consecutive pole at Charlotte Motor Speedway with a 161.223 miles per hour clocking.

An intense weather system and heavy rains crossed the Carolinas on Thursday, wiping out the second round of qualifying and all practice sessions. By Saturday afternoon, more than 6 inches of rain had fallen on the Speedway, forcing a two-week postponement for the fourth annual World Service Life 300 for NASCAR Late Model Sportsman cars.

Front row starters David Pearson (right) and Buddy Baker (left) lead the 40-car field on the pace lap for the 1976 National 500. Pearson and Baker each won four NASCAR Winston Cup races at Charlotte. Donnie Allison slew the giants in the 500-miler, driving a second entry from the lightly regarded Hoss Ellington stable to victory. CMS Archives

81

Bobby Allison (No. 12) drove an American Motors Matador during the 1977 NASCAR Winston Cup season. The car proved to be a bundle of problems as Allison failed to win a single race and only logged five top-5 finishes. The following year, Allison brought the Matador to Charlotte and won the sixth annual World Service Life 300. *Greg Fielden*

However, the weather broke in time for Sunday's 500-miler. Donnie Allison, riding a five-year winless famine, drove a Hoss Ellington Chevrolet into the lead 27 laps from the finish and held off Cale Yarborough to score his third Charlotte Motor Speedway triumph. It was a stunning upset, and it represented the first NASCAR Winston Cup victory for team owner Ellington, who had changed drivers with the celerity with which most teams changed tires. Immediately after the race ended, NASCAR officials carefully inspected the engine in the winning car. Initially, it measured over the 358-ci limit, but after a cooling-down period, it was declared legal by NASCAR officials.

During the tense post-race inspection, Ellington seemed unworried. "This car is legal. We left all our cheater stuff at Darlington," he cracked.

Ray Hendrick scored his second straight victory in the 300-mile Late Model Sportsman event before a disappointing crowd of 17,500. The event was run on Saturday, October 23, the day before the NASCAR Winston Cup race at Rockingham.

The accelerated expansion at Charlotte Motor Speedway continued in the early part of 1977 with the addition of 10,000 new grandstand seats and the paving of several access roads. Humpy Wheeler and his staff were geared for a record spectator turnout for the 18th annual World 600. "When Darrell Waltrip won at

Darlington, sales for the World 600 skyrocketed the next day," said Wheeler.

David Pearson won his eighth consecutive pole on Wednesday of race week, but rains hit the Speedway Thursday. "If you want to end a drought," Cale Yarborough observed, "then just schedule a race at Charlotte Motor Speedway." Rain had played havoc with the schedule the past two years.

Second-round of qualifying didn't begin until 7:30 p.m. on Thursday, and concluded at the cusp of nightfall.

Dean Combs captured first place in the NASCAR Baby Grand race on Friday and Harry Gant sped to victory in the 200-mile event for open-wheel Modifieds.

A standing-room only crowd of 115,000, including Grand Marshal Elizabeth Taylor and her sixth husband, John Warner, turned out in ideal weather conditions on race Sunday. Richard Petty thoroughly laced the star-studded field, leading 311 of the 400 laps. He racked up $35,000 in lap money and his total winnings of $69,550 established a new NASCAR Winston Cup Grand National record for a single-event payoff.

"I haven't changed my style," Petty said, "but when they're paying that kind of lap money, it makes a difference. So I try to adjust my style to fit the situation."

By October 1977, the first phase of an $18 million beautification and expansion project was already under way. "Our whole objective has been to make Charlotte Motor Speedway the showcase of major league stock car racing," said Humpy Wheeler, "and I believe this expansion will meet this goal."

Darrell Waltrip won the rain-shortened sixth annual World Service Life 300 for NASCAR Late Model Sportsman cars and Benny Parsons motored away from the field to impressively capture the 18th running of the NAPA National 500.

Parsons, driving the L. G. DeWitt–owned Chevrolet, had nearly lapped the entire field when he ran out of fuel in the 287th of 334 laps. By the time he coasted around the track and received service from his Jake Elder–led crew, Cale Yarborough had assumed command. Yet it took only 10 laps for Parsons to hustle past Yarborough, and he sprinted to a 19.5-second victory. "I didn't dominate this race, my car did," said Parsons. "The credit goes to Jake and the crew."

As the sun set on the Speedway grounds on October 9, 1977, with the skeleton of towering grandstands rising into a charcoal Carolina sky, it became clearly evident that Charlotte Motor Speedway, through strong judgment from the front office, had followed a steady trend from being conservative to becoming spectacular.

Sandy Dell greets Benny Parsons in Victory Lane after the 1977 NAPA National 500. Parsons drove L. G. DeWitt's Chevrolet to an overwhelming triumph, leading 250 of the 334 laps. He finished 19.2 seconds in front of runner-up Cale Yarborough, despite running out of gas late in the race. *CMS Archives*

CHAPTER 8

Skyward Expansion

1978 – 1980

Every enterprise must have its pioneer, a person willing to venture into the unknown with the courage of his convictions. Such a man is Olin Bruton Smith, chairman of the board at Charlotte Motor Speedway. Since he took over undisputed control of the mile-and-a-half facility, high-rise grandstands sprouted like flowers in a spring shower.

In the late 1970s the Charlotte Motor Speedway became the envy of every auto racing promoter.

Phase One of an $18 million expansion project began in late 1977 and by the following May, seating capacity had reached 81,357. "I knew back in 1959 when we first broke ground on this property what I dreamed Charlotte Motor Speedway would one day become," Smith said shortly before the 19th annual World 600. "I am very proud to look around today and see some of those dreams materializing. We've dedicated ourselves to making Charlotte Motor Speedway the best in the world. Phase One is just the beginning."

Perennial pole cat David Pearson, who won 11 consecutive poles at Charlotte from 1973 to 1978, leads the chase into turn one at the start of the 1978 World 600. The high-rise front stretch grandstands and the 17 air-conditioned corporate suites represented the completion of Phase One of the Speedway's $18-million expansion program. *CMS Archives*

Benny Parsons' Oldsmobile skids to a halt after clobbering the wall during the 1978 NAPA National 500. Parsons was second in the NASCAR Winston Cup point standings entering the prestigious 500-miler, but fell to fourth due to the bone-jarring mishap. *CMS photo by Bill Niven*

Dale Earnhardt (No. 98) and Dave Marcis (No. 2), teammates on the Rod Osterlund team, pair up in their Chevrolet Monte Carlos during the 1978 World Service Life 300. In his first effort with the Osterlund team, Earnhardt led seven times for 39 laps and very nearly won the race. The 27-year-old youngster held the lead until four laps from the finish and wound up second to Bobby Allison. Marcis came in third. *Greg Fielden*

Phase One included 10,000 high-rise grandstands along the front chute, an ultra-modern 150-seat press box fully equipped to handle the new computer age, 17 plush air-conditioned, enclosed corporate suites accommodating 1,500, a master control center perched atop the new structure, additional concession stands and restrooms, 30 additional acres for parking and a contemporary 14,000-square-foot administration building, a new ticket outlet building, and a 46-foot express elevator to the press/VIP area, the first elevator at a speedway since Ontario Motor Speedway opened in southern California in 1970.

"NASCAR Winston Cup stock car racing is reaching a totally new dimension and has become perhaps the fastest-growing professional sport in the United States," declared Smith, a promoter of indefatigable fortitude. "Charlotte is the center of this growth and Charlotte Motor Speedway has the responsibility of continuing the sport's rich tradition and heritage.

"Most stadiums are owned by municipalities and additions are usually financed through bonds or additional taxes, and the costs have been unbelievable. It doesn't have to be that way. We have proven that private capital, put to proper use, can finance large additional stadiums at nominal costs without sacrificing quality."

The projected appearance of Willy T. Ribbs, America's most celebrated African-American driver, gathered plenty of headlines during race week in May 1978. Ribbs was slated to drive a Ford owned by privateer Will Cronkrite and partially financed by the Speedway. Two days of private practice session were arranged so Ribbs, a top-notch sports car racer, could get acclimated to the heavier NASCAR stockers.

On Monday, May 16, 1978, Ribbs did not appear for the practice session. Instead, he was taking up temporary residence at the "Crossbar Hotel" (jail), as Willy T. put it. Ribbs was arrested by officers B. L. Stickley and T. W. Hopkins for going the wrong way on a one-way street in downtown Charlotte. Having missed the practice sessions, Cronkrite decided to replace Ribbs in the Ford he had obtained from Bud Moore. That replacement was a local kid by the name of Dale Earnhardt.

David Pearson snared his 10th straight pole position at Charlotte Motor Speedway. The swift ride netted Pearson and the Wood Brothers $15,000 from a record $30,000 in posted pole day awards. It was the first time since 1968 that a four-lap race against the clock had determined the front end of the starting field.

Rising star Darrell Waltrip slapped the wall in a practice session and missed the opening round of qualifying. Defending World 600 champ Richard Petty failed to pass technical inspection, and both Waltrip and Petty secured starting berths in the second day of time trials.

A double-header on Saturday featured the exotic Can-Am vehicles and a 100-mile event for NASCAR Late Model Sportsman cars. Elliott Forbes-Robinson won the 200-km Can-Am ace on the 2.25-mile road course and Morgan Shepherd took top honors in the Sportsman race.

Sunday's World 600 attracted a record crowd of 125,000, which collectively stood and cheered one of the most spine-tingling spectacles in auto racing. Six drivers swapped the lead 47 times and the 600-mile marathon event became a 4-hour, 20-minute trophy dash.

Six cars were in the hunt with fewer than two laps remaining. Waltrip held a narrow lead, with Donnie Allison and Benny Parsons waging a side-by-side duel for second place. Pearson was a close fourth with Bobby Allison and Cale Yarborough riding the leaders' tailpipes.

As Parsons swung to the high side to pass Donnie Allison, the two cars touched. Parsons' Oldsmobile cocked sideways, bounced off the wall, and collided with Pearson's Mercury. Waltrip breezed to victory as Allison recovered to finish second. Bobby Allison sneaked through the carnage to come home third. Yarborough took fourth while Pearson and Parsons got their crumpled mounts rolling again and finished fifth and sixth, respectively.

"I have never run so hard for so long to win a race," said Waltrip. "I've never seen that many cars running so equally late in the race. It would have been one heck of a finish if we had to race that last lap and a half."

Young Earnhardt, in his fifth career Winston Cup start, finished 17th with relief help from Harry Gant. Earnhardt returned to Charlotte Motor Speedway in October for the 19th annual NAPA National 500 in Cronkrite's Ford, but he also had a hot Late Model Sportsman car for the 300-mile World Service Life 300. Rod Osterlund, a wealthy Californian, gave the 27-year-old driver a seat in one of his potent Chevrolets for Saturday's Late Model show.

In that Saturday race Earnhardt qualified eighth and ran with the leaders all day. The crowd of 42,500 was clearly pulling for the local short-track artist, who regularly competed in area dirt track races. Earnhardt led in the closing stages, but Bobby Allison wheeled his American Motors Matador into first place with four laps remaining to beat Earnhardt by a single car length.

In Victory Lane, Allison delivered praise for the second-generation driver. "I want to congratulate Dale Earnhardt," said Allison. "He gave me all I could handle. He's fast becoming a very, very good race car driver."

Long-time Chrysler patron Richard Petty bagged his bulky Dodge Magnum midway through the 1978 season. The Petty Enterprises team brought a Chevrolet to Charlotte Motor Speedway for the 1978 NAPA National 500. The King led 102 of the first 217 laps, but ignition problems intervened and cost him at shot at the victory. *Greg Fielden*

Bobby Allison (No. 15) and David Pearson (No. 21) battle for the lead at Charlotte in 1978 in a pair of aerodynamically disadvantaged Ford Motor Company products. Allison appeared to be in a tailspin following two winless campaigns in 1976 and 1977. He hooked up with team owner Bud Moore in 1978 and won five races, including the NAPA National 500 at Charlotte and the Daytona 500. *Greg Fielden*

Veteran campaigner Hoss Ellington fielded a NASCAR Winston Cup team for 20 years. A who's who list of drivers saddled up in his No. 1 Chevrolet over the years, including such names as Fred Lorenzen, Davey Allison, David Pearson, Bobby Isaac, Neil Bonnett, Buddy Baker, Donnie Allison, and A. J. Foyt. Donnie Allison, pictured here during a pit stop at Charlotte, was the most successful; scoring four of the five wins the Ellington team recorded in NASCAR's elite series. *Greg Fielden*

Bill Elliott and his homespun family operation acquired a former Roger Penske Mercury in late 1977. While the big Mercury was nearly two years old when they took delivery of it, it was a step up for their independent team. Elliott showed tremendous promise while driving the former Penske machine, scoring three top-10 finishes at Charlotte. *Greg Fielden*

Allison came back the next day and prevailed in the 500-miler by a comfortable 30.2-second margin over Darrell Waltrip, who took the runner-up position when Dave Marcis ran out of fuel in the final lap.

Richard Petty, who had given up on the bulky Dodge Magnum midway through the 1978 season, drove a Chevrolet for the first time at Charlotte Motor Speedway. Petty led 102 laps before mechanical problems ended his day.

Cale Yarborough, who was en route to his third straight NASCAR championship, blew the engine in his Oldsmobile in the 206th lap. His Junior Johnson crew installed a new engine in 13 minutes, enabling Cale to salvage a 22nd place finish. NASCAR rules in 1978 permitted the change of engines during the running of the race.

Allison's weekend sweep was the first time any driver had won both Saturday's and Sunday's NASCAR events at Charlotte Motor Speedway.

The early part of the 1979 season proved to be a bonanza for the sport of stock car racing. The live flag-to-flag telecast of the Daytona 500 by CBS Sports was the first 500-mile NASCAR event broadcast in its entirety on a major network. Ratings for the Daytona 500 were an astounding 13.5 during the final half-hour of the race. Richard Petty ended his 19-month, 45-race winless streak as Cale Yarborough and Donnie Allison crashed in the final lap. As Petty crossed under the checkered flag inches ahead of Darrell Waltrip and A. J. Foyt, Cale and Donnie, along with Bobby Allison, were duking it out—literally— in the infield. It was a magical moment in the annals of sports. The electrifying finish whet the appetite of race fans, and the curve of trackside attendance started a sharp rise.

Added to the mix was rookie sensation Dale Earnhardt, whose sparkling effort in Charlotte's 300-mile Late Model Sportsman race in 1978 led to a full-time assignment with the Rod Osterlund Winston Cup team. The lad from Kannapolis, North Carolina, was thoroughly aggressive and coldly ferocious. He didn't mind putting a few nicks in the shapely bodywork of his Chevrolet in heavy-duty action, and he barged into prominence by winning the April 1, 1979, race at Bristol.

A week after Earnhardt's first NASCAR Winston Cup win, one of NASCAR's most formidable teams split up. David Pearson and the Wood Brothers parted ways following a sluggish start in 1979 and a pit mis-cue at Darlington. Together, they had won 43 times in seven years while running an abbreviated annual schedule. The announcement of the team's demise was earth-shattering. Neil Bonnett replaced Pearson in the familiar maroon-and-white Mercury, and he quickly responded by winning at Dover a week before the 20th annual World 600.

The unconsciously brave Bonnett was immediately placed in the pressure cooker when the teams checked into Charlotte Motor Speedway. Pearson had won 11 straight pole positions at the track and Bonnett was now under the gun to continue the streak.

Another interesting sideshow was the entry of Kyle Petty, the 18-year-old third-generation member of the Petty family. Young Kyle won the Daytona ARCA 200 the first time he ever strapped himself into a race car, and he was preparing to begin his Winston Cup career at Charlotte.

On Tuesday, May 16, Kyle crashed out of turn four in a practice session. The car was repaired and brought back to the track the following day, but he crashed it again on the backstretch in a horrendous accident. The car escaped Petty's control, whacked both outside and inside walls, and broke apart. The rear of the car was destroyed and the fuel cell was dislodged from the car. "I knew I was in trouble when I saw my own gas tank pass me on the track," cracked Kyle. His Winston Cup debut would have to wait until midsummer at Talladega.

Bonnett averaged 160.125 miles per hour in his four-lap qualification run to secure the 600 pole, giving the Wood Brothers their 12th in a row at Charlotte. Bonnett earned the adulation of his peers. Pearson, not entered in the 600, said, "He's got what it takes. I knew the car was capable."

Waltrip said, "For Neil to come through like that in this situation is miraculous."

Richard Petty delivered similar praise: "He wasn't the least bit erratic. He did a heckuva job considering the pressure he was under."

Saturday's 300-miler was a contest for NASCAR's new Grand American Series. Darrell Waltrip drove his Chevrolet Nova to victory ahead of John Anderson's Camaro before a crowd of 52,000.

On Sunday, another record crowd of at least 135,000 passed through the turnstiles to watch the most competitive 600-miler in stock car racing history. Fifty-nine official lead changes kept the audience on its collective feet, and Waltrip had to use every speck of his vast reservoir of talent to keep Richard Petty and Dale Earnhardt at bay in the final duel, as the two swapped possession of second place three times in the final lap.

"Those last 40 laps were the toughest I've ever run," said the winner. "It was a real mental strain."

Neil Bonnett's bid for victory ended when his engine blew on lap 252, but he came back to Charlotte Motor Speedway in October and won the pole for the

Darrell Waltrip steers his DiGard Racing No. 88 Chevrolet under Neil Bonnett in the 1979 World 600. The event produced a record 59 lead changes during the course of the 600-miler, an all-time record at the speedway that may never be approached. Bonnett was taking his fourth ride in the Wood Brothers Mercury. *Greg Fielden*

The NASCAR Late Model Sportsman drivers rarely complied with conventional procedure while negotiating the tricky high banks at Charlotte Motor Speedway. In the 1979 World Service Life 300, Lennie Pond (No. 50) has two wheels on the apron as he ducks under Tommy Hilbert (No. 54). Morgan Shepherd (No. 7) takes to the high side as French-Canadian driver Laurent Rioux looks for an opening. *Greg Fielden*

Cale Yarborough wheels Junior Johnson's Chevrolet down pit road after a quick stop in the 1979 NAPA National 500. Yarborough, one of NASCAR's hardest chargers, employed conservative tactics and rode home a lap ahead of the field. "Driving conservative is against my nature," Yarborough said. "But it was a battlefield out there and I just dodged the bullets. Circumstances dictated the way I drove today." *Greg Fielden*

Benny Parsons and Darrell Waltrip hook up in a speedy draft down the front chute at Charlotte Motor Speedway in the 1979 NAPA National 500. Parsons was driving for team owner M. C. Anderson, who entered NASCAR racing in 1976. Parsons finished sixth in the 500, then won at North Wilkesboro a week later, giving Anderson his first of 10 NASCAR Winston Cup victories as a team owner. *Greg Fielden*

NAPA National 500. He hustled around the mile-and-a-half tri-oval at 164.179 miles per hour, surpassing Cale Yarborough's track record of 162.162, which had stood for 10 years.

The third and fourth turns had been resurfaced since the World 600, which contributed to the record runs. Eight drivers topped the old qualifying record.

Darrell Waltrip held off Harry Gant to win the seventh annual World Service Life 300 on Saturday.

Cale Yarborough prevailed in Sunday's 500, coasting home a lap ahead of the field after leader Buddy Baker crashed with 55 laps remaining. Bobby Allison ran second, followed by Waltrip and Richard Petty. Waltrip held a 53-point advantage over Petty in the Winston Cup standings after the race, but Petty would rally and capture his seventh NASCAR title by a 12-point cushion.

The 1980 NASCAR Winston Cup season featured the usual top-rated teams gobbling up most of the attention. But they were being crowded by sophomore Dale Earnhardt, who won at Atlanta and Bristol and was leading the point standings when the tour arrived at Charlotte Motor Speedway in May.

One of the most enduring streaks came to a dramatic end during the opening round of qualifying for the 21st annual World 600. The Wood Brothers team had earned 13 consecutive poles at Charlotte Motor Speedway, but Neil Bonnett could only muster the fifth-fastest speed as Cale Yarborough posted quick time. David Pearson, who landed a ride with Hoss Ellington a few weeks earlier, nabbed the outside front row starting position.

"We knew it had to end sometime," said Leonard Wood, crew chief for the Stuart, Virginia–based team. "We gave it a good shot, but Cale and Junior [Johnson, team owner] gave it a better one."

Pearson prevailed in Saturday's Mello Yello 300 NASCAR Grand American race, outrunning the field by nearly a full lap.

Despite only a 30 percent chance of rain on Sunday for the 600, persistent afternoon showers twice interrupted the race, forcing two red-flag delays that totaled nearly two hours. In between the showers, officials waved a record 14 caution flags consuming 114 laps, and some terrific racing as six drivers swapped the lead 47 times.

In the 276th lap, Pearson, Yarborough, Earnhardt, and Bobby Allison tangled while challenging leaders Benny Parsons and Darrell Waltrip. All but Allison continued, but the mishap reduced the furious pace to two cars. Parsons muscled his way past Waltrip with two laps remaining and held off his rival by a single car length at the finish line. The race ended at 6:40 p.m.

"It was thrilling just to be a part of a great finish," said Parsons, who had finished second in three of the last six races. "You can't understand how depressing it is to keep getting so doggone close and coming away with nothing. We needed this victory awful bad. Maybe our depression will go away."

Team owner M. C. Anderson enjoyed basking in Victory Lane for only the third time in his career. "A lot of people are happy with second-place finishes, but we aren't," said the Savannah, Georgia, construction magnate. "Second is still losing. I'd just as soon finish 30th."

The day after the World 600, Jake Elder, Earnhardt's crew chief, suddenly quit the Osterlund team. His departure was expected to put a crimp in Earnhardt's championship aspirations. Twenty-year-old rookie crew chief Doug Richert was named as replacement. The shake-up within the Osterlund team did not have any negative effects on Earnhardt's performance, as he maintained his point lead throughout the summer. Entering the National 500, he held a 105-point lead over Yarborough.

Yarborough and Earnhardt earned starting positions in the second row as Buddy Baker and independent Ricky Rudd nailed down the front row.

The 300-mile NASCAR Late Model Sportsman race on Saturday was a bizarre contest won by Dave Marcis. The race ended under the yellow flag as a wild crash six laps from the finish sent Dale Jarrett to the hospital with a fractured ankle. Gene Glover was treated for bruises after his car tumbled six times in the mishap.

The pace car went onto the track to pick up the leaders, but spun in the oil deposited by Glover and darted into the path of Geoff Bodine's Pontiac, which had been running fifth. The cars collided, knocking the pace car out of action. Bodine dropped to 11th in the final rundown. Ironically, the incident was the second in two weeks involving the pace car. Two weeks earlier at North Wilkesboro, the pace car crashed into a parked vehicle when entering pit road.

Chilly temperatures and a few flakes of snow greeted the crowd of 75,000 on Sunday morning, but action was hot and heavy on the track. Title contenders Earnhardt and Yarborough, along with nine other drivers, traded the lead 43 times. Earnhardt led 12 times for 143 laps, including the final 44, and edged Yarborough by 1.83 seconds. It was the fifth win of the season for Earnhardt and his first in his home state of North Carolina.

"No one can know how much I've dreamed and thought about this moment," said an emotional Earnhardt. "It's an even better feeling than I thought it would be."

Earnhardt went on to capture the 1980 NASCAR Winston Cup championship by 19 points over Yarborough, becoming the first driver to ever win Rookie of the Year and the national driving title in successive seasons.

The landscape of NASCAR was changing with the times. The 1980 season was the final one in which full-bodied cars graced the high-banked speedways. Following the trend in America, smaller cars were utilized for NASCAR's premier series effective in 1981.

A cut tire on Dale Earnhardt's No. 2 Chevrolet triggered a big crash in the 1980 World 600, taking contenders David Pearson (No. 1), Cale Yarborough (No. 11), and Bobby Allison out of the hunt for victory. The crash opened the door for Benny Parsons, who prevailed after a spirited duel with Darrell Waltrip in the final laps. *CMS Archives*

Buddy Baker pitches his Ranier Racing Buick into the first turn during the 1980 National 500. Baker started on the pole and finished a strong third. David Pearson, Benny Parsons, Neil Bonnett, Darrell Waltrip, and Richard Petty are in hot pursuit. *CMS Archives*

CHAPTER 9

Small Cars, Old Pros, and Diamonds in the Rough

1981–1982

Since 1976, the NASCAR hierarchy was aware that the use of smaller American-made automobiles in the Winston Cup Series would eventually become a necessity. The automobile manufacturers, faced with the continuing rise in fuel shortages and steeper crude oil prices, were producing smaller cars for the American public. While the nation's streets were filled with midsize cars, the full-bodied monsters still graced the high-banked speedways. "Eventually, we will have to follow Detroit's lead," admitted NASCAR president Bill France, Jr.

The transition from 115-inch wheelbase cars to trimmed-down models with 110-inch wheelbases took five years of planning and gradual and deliberate legislation. By 1981 new rules set by the sanctioning body placed virtually all NASCAR Winston Cup teams back at square one. With the influx of small-bodied Winston Cup cars for the 1981 season, NASCAR teams found themselves scrambling to stock their shops with new sheet metal, searching for the appropriate chassis setup, and preparing for the venture into an uncharted domain.

Darrell Waltrip (No. 11) and Dale Earnhardt (No. 15) bring their mounts in for pit service. Waltrip won 24 NASCAR Winston Cup races during the 1981 and 1982 seasons; his first two years driving for Junior Johnson. Waltrip's Mountain Dew Buick was clearly the class of the series and he won the championship both years. *CMS Archives*

Bobby Allison joined the Harry Ranier–owned team for the 1981 NASCAR Winston Cup campaign. Starting the season in a fleet but controversial Pontiac Grand Prix, Allison and his Waddell Wilson–led team switched to a Buick in April after rule changes rendered the Pontiac uncompetitive. The team went on a midseason roll, winning three of seven events including the World 600. The Victory Lane ceremony was filled with virtually every member of the Ranier team. *CMS Archives*

Flamboyant and devil-may-care Gary Balough, who honed his raucous talents on the adventurous short tracks, applied his rambunctious trade on the high banks of the Speedway in the 1981 Miller High Life 300 Late Model Sportsman race. Balough made a breathtaking pass for the lead, sliding past Jody Ridley (No. 98) and Mark Martin (No. 02) late in the race. Balough went on to win the thrilling contest but was lambasted by other drivers for his relentless driving techniques. *CMS photo by David Allio*

While the cars proved to be less stable—Daytona's Speedweeks was punctuated with a series of horrific crashes—the action on the track was wide open. Huge packs of cars toured the high-banked speedways at breakneck speeds, producing perhaps the most enlightening and entertaining speed contests ever seen.

There were 49 lead changes in the Daytona 500 and 35 in the summer 400-miler. Lead changes at the two Rockingham races numbered 36 and 33; Talladega had 43 and 39 lead changes during its two annual events; and the two events at the 2-mile Michigan oval produced 65 and 47 lead changes, respectively. Eleven of the Winston Cup races had 10 or more different leaders. During the 31-race 1981 season, 772 official lead changes took place, an all-time record that remains unsurpassed today. Statistical numbers skyrocketed and so did the attendance, as fans clamored to watch the helmeted NASCAR gladiators carve a new niche in the adventurous realms of a rapidly changing speed game.

Charlotte Motor Speedway's spring calendar offered a variety of events. A Sports Car Club of America (SCCA) Trans Am race conducted on the 2.25-mile road course was won by Canadian Eppie Wietzes. Al Unser, Jr., 18-year-old member of the famous Albuquerque, New Mexico, clan, prevailed in the Super Vee event, and Don Knowles won the Rabbit race for Volkswagen automobiles.

Lean Richard Petty relaxes in the garage area at the Speedway before the 1981 Miller High Life 500. The acknowledged King of stock car racing had won 195 NASCAR Winston Cup races entering the event. It would take him nearly three years to complete the sojourn to the magic 200-victory plateau. *CMS Archives*

Three-time Indianapolis 500 winner Johnny Rutherford competed in 35 NASCAR Winston Cup races from 1963 to 1988. His most active year was 1981, when he drove in a dozen events for team owner Dr. Ron Benfield. A blown engine caused him to spin in the 1981 Miller High Life 500. Midwestern ace Bob Senneker (No. 6), driving in his first Winston Cup race since 1970, scoots by safely to the high side. *CMS Archives*

The deep-throated NASCAR stockers checked in on Tuesday, May 19, 1981, for the 22nd running of the World 600. Bobby Allison entered the race with a comfortable 168-point lead over Ricky Rudd, who replaced Darrell Waltrip in the DiGard car. Waltrip, who bought out his contract with DiGard and moved to the Junior Johnson team, ranked third in the standings, 207 points behind Allison.

Dale Earnhardt was mired in a slump. Despite his terrific championship season in 1980, Earnhardt and his Rod Osterlund team had gone winless through May.

Morgan Shepherd wheeled his Pontiac Ventura to victory in Saturday's Mello Yello 300. Leading for 150 of the 200 laps, Shepherd held a 12-second advantage over Earnhardt when a late crash forced the event to end under the caution flag.

Another sellout crowd turned out in warm, sunny weather to watch the 1981 edition of the world's longest NASCAR Winston Cup event. Neil Bonnett led the opening lap from the pole, then Earnhardt charged

David Pearson's 14th and final pole at Charlotte came in qualifying for the 1982 World 600. Driving a Buick owned by sophomore team owner Bobby Hawkins, the highly revered "Silver Fox" turned in a mild surprise on pole day to earn the premier starting spot. Flanking Pearson on the front row is Buddy Baker. Pearson and Baker combined for eight wins on the Charlotte mile-and-a-half. *CMS Archives*

Kyle Petty's colorful STP Pontiac dives into the first turn ahead of a pack of cars in the 1982 World 600. The 1982 edition of the world's longest stock car race was one of the hottest on record as temperatures soared into the mid-90s Fahrenheit. Young Petty was overcome by the heat midway through the event, and Tim Richmond brought the car home in 17th position. *CMS Archives*

from his fifth starting position to lead the next 35 trips. After pacing himself during the early going, Bonnett unleashed the power of his Wood Brothers steed and opened a comfortable lead. In the 152nd lap, Donnie Allison lost control of his Oldsmobile in the fourth turn, banged into the wall, and slid directly into the path of an onrushing Buick manned by Dick Brooks. The two cars hit passenger side to passenger side.

Allison was knocked unconscious in the collision, and Brooks had a painful shoulder injury. Allison was lifted from his car and transported to Charlotte Memorial Hospital, suffering a broken right shoulder blade, a concussion, fractured ribs, a bruised right lung, and a broken left knee. He was placed in the intensive care unit and listed in "guarded" condition.

Bonnett was eliminated in another scary crash on lap 210. With the caution flag in the air, Bonnett was racing back to the stripe in an effort to keep Cale Yarborough a lap behind. As the speeding pair hustled toward the start-finish line, Bonnett plowed into the lapped car of Bobby Wawak. Bonnett veered off the track and struck the inside pit barrier just past the exit of pit road. Groggily, he climbed from the demolished car.

Bobby Allison, driving Harry Ranier's Buick, led the final 70 laps and outran Harry Gant by 8.2 seconds. "My heart was in my throat all afternoon since I saw Donnie was in a bad wreck," said a subdued Allison in Victory Lane. "I could put it out of my mind when we were running under green. Had to. But it really bothered me when we slowed down under yellow." It was Allison's fifth Winston Cup triumph at Charlotte Motor Speedway.

When the tour returned to Charlotte for the 22nd annual National 500, Dale Earnhardt was still winless and had switched teams. Rod Osterlund had suddenly and unexpectedly sold his operation to J. D. Stacy in June. By August, Earnhardt had stepped out of the ride and landed with independent Richard Childress, who promptly retired as driver when Earnhardt became available.

Darrell Waltrip and Bobby Allison were locked in a ferocious duel for the Winston Cup title. Waltrip trailed by a 341-point margin in June, but went on a tear, finishing no worse than third during a 10-race stretch. Allison's lead had disappeared by September, and he trailed Waltrip by 53 points entering the National 500.

Saturday's Miller 300, run under cool, overcast skies, was an electrifying, nonstop escapade of fender rubbing and thunderbolt action. The crowd of about 30,000 was treated to a devouring slugfest in which emancipated short-track specialist Gary Balough prevailed over 41 other steaming and outspoken rivals.

Youthful and spirited newcomers Terry Labonte (No. 44) and Rusty Wallace (No. 72) battle through the first turn during the 1982 World 600. Both Labonte and Wallace would eventually rise to the pinnacle of their profession and reign as NASCAR Winston Cup champions. *CMS Archives*

Balough led the final 24 laps and beat runner-up Mark Martin by 1.3 seconds. In the garage area after the race, the focus was clearly on Balough and his unrestrained method of getting to the front without flinching. Along the way, he ruffled the feathers of many hardened veterans.

Said pole-sitter Jody Ridley: "I've been racing for 16 years, and that's the dirtiest [expletive deleted] I've ever seen in a race car."

Earnhardt, a highly charged racer who was compiling a repertoire of on-track shenanigans himself, declared, "That boy in the 75 car [Balough] needs a lesson in how to drive on a superspeedway. That ain't no way to race."

Balough defended his unabated driving style. "Nobody on the track abused me intentionally, and I didn't abuse anybody else intentionally," said the 34-year-old Floridian. "We were racing. What else can I tell you?"

Title contenders Waltrip and Allison held center stage during the Sunday's 500 and finished first and second, respectively, in another caution-riddled event. The yellow flag was out for a total of 78 laps, reducing Waltrip's winning average speed to 117.483 miles per hour, the slowest autumn event at Charlotte Motor Speedway since Speedy Thompson's 112.760 miles per hour clip in the 1960 inaugural 400-miler.

Waltrip ended the season with 17 consecutive top 10 finishes and won his first NASCAR Winston Cup championship by 53 points over Allison.

Waltrip and Allison were also near the front of the point standings in 1982, having posted seven victories collectively in the season's first 11 races. Entering the 23rd annual World 600, upstart Terry Labonte was atop the standings with Waltrip and Allison in pursuit.

David Pearson, seated in a lightly regarded Buick entered by Bobby Hawkins, pulled off his 14th pole for a major Charlotte Motor Speedway race with a speed of 162.511 miles per hour.

Sanctioning NASCAR developed a stabilized series for the Late Model Sportsman drivers in 1982. The series point championship had previously been determined by a potpourri of short-track events, weekly contests, and an occasional superspeedway event. In 1982 a point system similar to the Winston Cup was put into

Dave Marcis cocks his Buick sideways in front of Neil Bonnett and Ricky Rudd during a furious battle in the 1982 World 600. Marcis came out of the slide and went on to finish ninth. Bonnett won the race and Rudd wound up seventh. *CMS Archives*

the race Bill drove. His talent really showed today."

Elliott, weakened by the torturous heat, flopped down on the wooden bench in the garage area. "I always thought I could drive a race car," he said. "Today sort of proved to me I wasn't being foolish."

By the time the tour returned to Charlotte Motor Speedway for the 23rd annual National 500, Allison and Waltrip were locked in another terrific struggle for the NASCAR Winston Cup championship. Waltrip rallied from a sizable midseason deficit and was trailing by only 15 points.

Harry Gant and Geoff Bodine earned front row starting slots in pole qualifying for the 500 on Wednesday. The next day, they repeated their feat during time trials for the Miller 300 Late Model Sportsman event. Moments after Gant celebrated his second pole in as many days, however, NASCAR announced that both runs by Gant (164.129 miles per hour) and Bodine (163.905) had been disallowed, and that Phil Parsons' effort of 162.191 miles per hour inherited the pole. Sanctioning NASCAR declared the carburetors on the two Pontiacs to be illegal, and both would have to requalify on Friday. The mild-mannered Gant was exasperated. "NASCAR checked and sealed the carburetor this morning. It was still sealed after qualifying. If it was OK then, it's gotta be OK now," he said. "It's the same carburetor I won the Mello Yello 300 with here in May. It was legal then and it hasn't changed."

Heavy rains washed out all track activity on Friday, leaving Gant and Bodine—along with Dale Earnhardt and Mark Martin, who did not post a time on Thursday—unable to log official qualifying times. All four were unable to start the 300.

Before a crowd of 51,000, Waltrip wheeled his Pontiac to a 1.8-second victory over Late Model Sportsman regular Sam Ard, after top contenders Morgan Shepherd and Phil Parsons encountered late race problems.

Sunday's National 500 was conducted under heavily overcast skies and cool temperatures, which kept the crowd down to about 65,000. Gant led the opening 19 laps from the pole but took a back seat to Bobby Allison's fleet DiGard Racing Buick. Gant nearly fell from contention when he cut a tire and spun on

Bill Elliott, driving the No. 9 Melling Ford, made a most impressive run in the 1982 World 600. Starting 14th on the grid, Elliott picked off his more powerful rivals methodically and battled veteran Neil Bonnett for the victory. Bonnett, wheeling the Wood Brothers No. 21 Ford, dashed past Elliott with 13 laps remaining and prevailed in a spine-tingling finish. CMS Archives

effect. After a sparkling duel that had a crowd of 62,500 on its feet, Harry Gant nipped Dale Earnhardt and Morgan Shepherd at the finish line to win the Mello Yello 300.

Heat was a major factor in Sunday's World 600. Temperatures spiraled into the mid-90s with a humidity to match. Speedway President Humpy Wheeler said the unbearable conditions forced him to "shut off the infield to automobiles earlier than usual this morning. It's less than capacity. Cost about $25,000 in revenue, but we have all roads open in case we have an emergency."

Several fans were treated for heat-related ailments and several drivers sought the assistance of relief drivers, but emergencies were avoided. Neil Bonnett and relative newcomer Bill Elliott forged to the front in a steamy display of speed and stamina in the waning laps of the 600. Elliott, bidding for his first career Winston Cup victory, poked the nose of his Harry Melling–owned Ford ahead with 41 laps to go and kept Bonnett at bay for 28 laps.

With just 13 laps remaining, Bonnett ducked under Elliott as they whipped off the fourth corner and held the lead to the finish. Elliott trailed by two car lengths at the flag. "It was so hot today," said Bonnett. "There at the last, every time I breathed it was like swallowing fire. I tried to make the back of my little 'Bird 60 feet wide that last lap. I can't say enough good things about

lap 231. He recovered, pitted under caution for fresh rubber, and managed to stay on the lead lap.

On the restart, Allison and Bill Elliott were racing for the lead while Richard Petty, one lap down, and Dale Earnhardt, two laps down, were trying to unlap themselves. Earnhardt and Petty tangled as the pack sped into the third turn, setting off a wild, 10-car melee that included Waltrip's Buick. After numerous pit stops, Waltrip continued at a reduced speed.

Allison was the horse of the field, leading for 280 of the 334 laps. Well within the shadow of the checkered flag, his Buick popped an engine with 10 laps remaining. Elliott assumed command as the caution came out. Gant, the only other driver in the lead lap, pitted for four new tires while Elliott waited until the last lap of yellow to make a quick pit stop for two tires.

The green came out with four laps to go and Gant sailed uncontested to his first triumph on a superspeedway. "I almost couldn't keep from crying those last two laps," said Gant. "That's how much this means to me."

Championship contenders Allison and Waltrip wound up 9th and 14th, respectively, allowing Allison to cushion his lead slightly in the point standings. But by the time the 1982 season had closed under a blue California sky at Riverside, Waltrip had rallied once again and won his second consecutive Winston Cup title by 72 points.

CHAPTER 10

Big Plans, Hot Action, and Homes on the Range

1983–1984

In the early 1980s, NASCAR Winston Cup racing had an appeal too tempting for millions of motorsports enthusiasts to resist. The violent thunder, blessed with aesthetic charm when the green flag unfurled, beckoned audiences in record numbers. Sunday after Sunday, the battle was a new one—and another chance for glory on the steeply pitched pavement of NASCAR's expansive domain. The races themselves, by virtue of the time of season and the importance of the point standings, developed their own special characters.

Darrell Waltrip and Bobby Allison, in their annual struggles for Winston Cup supremacy, captivated race fans across the globe. Stylish veterans such as Richard Petty, Cale Yarborough, Neil Bonnett, Buddy Baker, and David Pearson, along with flashy newcomers like Dale Earnhardt, Bill Elliott, Terry Labonte, Tim Richmond, and Ricky Rudd, combined to unfold an exciting odyssey in American motorsports.

Harry Gant and Benny Parsons lead the charge into the first turn moments after the start of the 1984 World 600. The 40-unit condominiums were completed in time for residents to watch the NASCAR Winston Cup race from the comfort of their living rooms. *CMS Archives*

Charlotte Motor Speedway was on the cusp of another major expansion to accommodate the rapidly growing numbers of ticket buyers. By May of 1983, 12,000 new individual galvanized chair seats had been assembled and installed in the upper rows along the front stretch grandstands. A new infield media center had been christened, and other refinements were in order for the May extravaganza.

Joining the NASCAR Winston Cup stockers in 1983 were the exotic International Motorsports Association (IMSA) Camel GT prototype sports cars, which competed in a 500-km race on May 16, 1983. The duo of Al Holbert and Jim Trueman co-drove a new Porsche to victory on the infield road course before an enthusiastic and larger-than-expected crowd of 62,000.

The 24th annual World 600 contained the backdrop of a recurring mirrored image. Bobby Allison was atop the Winston Cup standings with a pack of rivals giving chase, including his nemesis Darrell Waltrip, who was logged in seventh place, 208 points behind.

Buddy Baker placed the Wood Brothers Ford on the pole for the 600—an upset, considering it was only the third pole in two calendar years for the Dearborn nameplate. Bill Elliott, still looking for his first major league victory, earned the second starting spot. Allison and Waltrip occupied the seventh row.

Winston Cup drivers dominated Saturday's Mello Yello 300, leading all but three of the 200 laps. Dale Earnhardt, driving a Pontiac maintained by Robert Gee, led 63 laps en route to victory in the 300-miler. Winston Cuppers Neil Bonnett, Bill Elliott, Harry Gant, and Bobby Allison rounded out the top five.

A crowd of 137,000-plus filled the Charlotte Motor Speedway grounds on Sunday for the 1983 World 600. Earnhardt led the opening 18 laps, getting the jump from his second row starting berth. Bobby Allison knifed his way through the contenders and took the lead in the 19th lap. Allison's Buick scampered away from its rivals, with only Bill Elliott able to keep Allison in sight.

Darrell Waltrip steers through the high banks ahead of Bill Elliott as D.K. Ulrich straddles the low groove in the 1983 World 600. Elliott was in a position to win his first NASCAR Winston Cup event, leading on three occasions for 47 laps, but was gobbled up in a big crash and fell from contention. Waltrip finished in fourth place in the race eventually won by Neil Bonnett. CMS Archives

Neil Bonnett became the third man to win back-to-back World 600s in 1982 and 1983. His victory in 1983 came in a Chevrolet owned by Butch Mock and Bob Rahilly. While the triumph was Bonnett's 12th in the NASCAR Winston Cup series, it was the first for Floridians Mock and Rahilly. Mock had been the team's original driver in 1978. CMS photo by Graham Niven

Allison led a total of 188 out of the 400 laps, and lapped every car in the field except Elliott's Ford when the fickle hand of fate intervened. Rookie Sterling Marlin cut a tire and looped his Chevrolet in the fourth turn on lap 342. Allison, approaching rapidly, applied his brakes. Elliott ran into the back of Slick Johnson, pushing Johnson into Allison. Elliott and Allison spun into the grassy area that separates the front stretch from the pit area. Allison continued with little delay while Elliott's crew spent 16 laps replacing a broken oil cooler.

Neil Bonnett and Richard Petty were able to get back into the lead lap during the melee. Bonnett took the lead for keeps with 53 laps and beat Petty by a couple of car lengths. Allison wound up in third place.

On June 23, 1983, Speedway chairman Bruton Smith announced an ambitious and accelerated $30 million expansion project, which would begin immediately. "This expansion will afford our fans and corporate sponsors the best possible environment for a

variety of motorsports events," said Smith, making the announcement at Charlotte's Radisson Plaza.

Included in the first phase was a new main entrance off U.S. Highway 29, 12,000 new grandstand seats, a new parking lot able to accommodate 5,000 automobiles, a new entrance tunnel located near the fourth turn, and a unique 40-unit condominium complex perched high atop the first turn grandstands.

The floor plans for each 1,100-square-foot unit would include two bedrooms, one and a half baths, and a full-length glass window overlooking the Speedway for a panoramic view of the racing action. The complex included a high-speed elevator, maximum security devices, private parking, and closed circuit television. Smith said the price for the condominiums would begin at $120,000.

Both corporate and non-corporate buyers purchased the units, a solid investment in the future of auto racing. "With the tremendous growth we are expecting today in stock car racing, we at Charlotte Motor Speedway believe the track facilities should grow as well," Smith said. "Our sport is the largest attended in the country and the attendance will continue to grow. With that in mind, we are beginning construction now to keep pace with the growth so Charlotte Motor Speedway will always be able to accommodate our fans in a first-class fashion."

Track president and general manager Humpy Wheeler said that the recent flurry of sell-outs had posed some not unpleasant dilemmas. "Obviously, we're in a sell-out situation for the World 600," said Wheeler. "We're missing a lot of sales because of the demand for premium seats. I'm sure we've lost 15,000

to 20,000 sales this year because we couldn't give the fans the seats they wanted. We're just going to have to tear up our original $18 million expansion plan and start over."

The Charlotte Motor Speedway continued to develop its corporate sector as well. Seventeen new suites, bringing the total to 42, extended down to the fourth turn. "We tread a difficult line of developing the corporate potential while offering the maximum service to fans," said Smith. "We think we do that better than any sports facility in the world."

The expansion was in full gear when the NASCAR Winston Cuppers arrived for the 24th annual Miller High Life 500 in October. Bobby Allison held

Morgan Shepherd leads the chase into the first turn in the opening lap of the 1983 Miller Time 300 NASCAR Late Model Sportsman race. Shepherd was the class of the field, leading for 149 of the first 179 laps. With victory in sight, the engine in Shepherd's Oldsmobile failed, opening the door for Sam Ard to post his first big-track victory. *CMS Archives*

Sam Ard, in the Thomas Brothers No. 00 Oldsmobile, shown dueling with Geoff Bodine and Lake Speed, was a regular in the Saturday Late Model Sportsman events. The lanky short track artist drove to victory in the 1983 Miller Time 300, his first win on a super speedway. The triumph also made up for ill fortune that struck him 10 years earlier at Charlotte Motor Speedway. Ard had been in the hunt for the NASCAR Late Model Sportsman championship in 1973, but crashed on the second lap of the inaugural Saturday event. As a result, he lost his ride with Thomas Brothers. Several years later, Ard was back in the saddle of the No. 00. He reached the pinnacle in 1983 by taking the series championship and won it again in 1984. *CMS Archives*

Dale Earnhardt loops his Bud Moore Ford in the fourth turn in the 1983 Miller High Life 500 as Darrell Waltrip and Buddy Baker sail past the incident. Earnhardt had led the 500 on two previous occasions, but fell two laps off the pace after the spin and wound up 14th. Earnhardt drove the Bud Moore Ford in 1982 and 1983, winning three races during his tenure with the veteran team owner. CMS Archives

Richard Petty flashes his patented smile from Victory Lane after winning the 1983 Miller Time 500. It was the 198th career win for the King of stock car racing, but the joyous occasion turned sour when, in a post-race inspection, NASCAR officials discovered both improper tires on the car and an oversized engine. CMS Archives

a 96-point lead over Darrell Waltrip in the Winston Cup standings, and another down-to-the-wire battle for the championship was in the making between two of NASCAR's most revered competitors.

In one of the most perplexing marketing bonanzas to strike the sport in years, Tim Richmond drove the Old Milwaukee Pontiac into the Busch pole position for the Miller High Life 500. Richmond, driving for drag racing kingpin Raymond Beadle, tied four laps together at a record average speed of 163.073 miles per hour.

In the Miller Time 300 for NASCAR Late Model Sportsman cars, Sam Ard, a 44-year-old short-track artist who had never found the right path to make it to the Winston Cup Series, produced a popular upset. Driving an Oldsmobile based out of Asheboro, North Carolina, Ard took the lead with 22 laps remaining and outran Dale Earnhardt to score the biggest win of his career. It was the first win for a Late Model Sportsman driver in the 300 since Ray Hendrick had prevailed in 1976.

A powerful field was ready for the Miller High Life 500. Richard Petty, still looking to inch closer to the magic 200-victory mark, had been stuck on 197 since Talladega in May. He had qualified his Pontiac in 20th place, but was well off the pace of the front-runners. In what became known as the Pettygate affair, King Richard lumbered around on the lead lap the entire day, but never challenged for the lead—until the final pit stop.

The final caution flag ended with 37 laps remaining, and Petty, deep in the field, turned up the wick. He carved his way through the pack, sped around Darrell Waltrip with 23 laps to go, and set sail. Petty was untouchable in the final 40 miles, extending his lead to 3.1 seconds when the checkered flag fell. Waltrip finished second, trimming Allison's point lead to 67 points.

After Petty went through the victory ceremonies, NASCAR technical director Bill Gazaway delivered an announcement in the press box. "Officially, right now, the finish of the event is unofficial."

Gazaway and his troops had discovered that Petty's engine had a piston displacement of 381.983 ci, nearly 24 more than the 358 maximum permitted. Not only that, but left-side tires of a soft rubber compound had been placed on the right side of Petty's STP Pontiac during the final pit stop. The softer compound improves speed on short runs at the sacrifice of durability.

After a lengthy consultation among high-ranking NASCAR officials, the sanctioning body allowed Petty to keep his 198th career victory but hit King Richard with a record $35,000 fine and docked him 104 championship points. "We had several options at our disposal," said Gazaway in making the official decision as darkness descended over the Speedway. "We took what we felt like [were] our best options in determining these penalties. The rationale, the whys and what-have-you is that's that—and that's the end of the discussion."

Petty claimed he was unaware of the illegalities when he made his valiant charge in the waning laps.

Pole-sitter Benny Parsons pitches his No. 55 into the first turn at the start of the 1984 Miller High Life 500. The field has already fanned out in three-abreast formation in the frenzied opening moments of the event. Parsons led seven times for 154 laps and finished second to Bill Elliott. *CMS Archives*

Terry Labonte, in his seventh year of NASCAR Winston Cup competition, drove Billy Hagan's No. 44 Piedmont Airlines Chevrolet to the Winston Cup title in 1984. Labonte, a model of consistency throughout his career, parlayed a cool head and iron nerve into his first two championships. In 1984, he won twice, scored 17 top-5 finishes, and 24 top-10 efforts in 30 starts during the exhaustive campaign. *CMS Archives*

"I didn't know what was going on. Business is getting away from me. And as I get further and further from the car, I become only the driver. I've been telling the crew I needed more horsepower. I guess they took me at my word," he said.

Petty went into the 1984 season two victories shy of 200 and Allison was the defending Winston Cup champion, having bagged his first NASCAR title. Petty scored win number 199 at Dover on May 20, 1984, and set up a promotional blitz for the Silver Anniversary running of the World 600. "Richard's 199th win adds that charge, that electric charge, that makes a big event doubly exciting," said Humpy Wheeler.

The same day Petty won at Dover, the IMSA races competed at Charlotte Motor Speedway before a series record 84,575 spectators. Bill Whittington and Randy Lanier combined to win the 500-km event for Camel GT cars.

Fifteen drivers turned in qualifying efforts on Wednesday before rain postponed the conclusion of pole day until Thursday. Cale Yarborough had been quickest on Wednesday, but cooler, cloudy conditions on Thursday afforded higher speed, and Yarborough wound up starting 14th. Harry Gant won the pole at 162.496 miles per hour.

The Mello Yello 300 was one of the most exciting events in Speedway history with Bobby Allison nosing out Darrell Waltrip by 18 inches. Lake Speed tagged at their heels in third place after a dive onto the grass foiled his efforts to make a slingshot pass off the final corner. A crowd of 87,000 cheered wildly at the heart-thumping finish.

After the race, Bruton Smith, citing "the tremendous competition," announced bonuses of $2,000 for Allison, Waltrip, and Speed, and $1,000 for Ron Bouchard, who had led 102 laps before engine failure put him on the sidelines. "This is the greatest Sportsman race ever run," said a jubilant Smith. "I know NASCAR discourages bonus money after the fact, but those guys put on such a good show that I'm giving it to them anyway."

A crowd estimated at 149,000 watched as Allison come back the following day and took his sixth victory at Charlotte Motor Speedway in the World 600. Allison grabbed the lead when the engine in Cale Yarborough's Chevrolet expired with 18 laps remaining. Dale Earnhardt came from 19th starting position to finish second.

Dale Earnhardt, a descendant of a family with strong warrior traditions, hooked up with team owner Richard Childress in 1984 following a two-year stint with Bud Moore. While Earnhardt drove for Childress in 11 races in 1981, the reunion laid the groundwork for the most prosperous partnership in NASCAR's modern times. Together Earnhardt and Childress have won six Winston Cup championships. *CMS Archives*

Cale Yarborough leads Bobby Allison in the dramatic stretch duel in the 1984 World 600. Yarborough, bidding for his first win in the 600-miler, was foiled by engine problems in the final 20 laps. Allison drove his DiGard Buick into the lead with 19 laps remaining and finished a half-lap ahead of runner-up Dale Earnhardt to score his sixth Winston Cup victory at Charlotte. *CMS photo by Jeffrey S. Johnson*

Richard Petty earned the eighth starting position, but a blown engine midway through the race ended his bid for win number 200. He was able to etch his name into the history books by scoring win number 200 in the July 4 Daytona 400 before a sun-bathed holiday crowd and with President Ronald Reagan in attendance.

Gant and Terry Labonte were battling for the 1984 NASCAR Winston Cup championship in October. Labonte, winner at Riverside and Bristol, was 91 points ahead of Gant, who had won three of the last eight races and was on a roll. Perennial contenders Darrell Waltrip and Bobby Allison were out of the immediate chase.

Benny Parsons drove his Johnny Hayes–owned Chevrolet into the pole position for the 25th anniversary running of the Miller High Life 500 with a four-lap average speed of 165.579. His run for the four qualifying laps was remarkably consistent: 165.568, 165.604, 165.578, and 165.568. The first and last laps were identical. "I have no idea how we ran so consistently," said Parsons after his 19th career pole. "I do know I couldn't be more delighted."

Darrell Waltrip won the Miller 300 NASCAR Late Model Sportsman race, having used all his savvy to hold off upstart Phil Parsons and Sam Ard in a three-car finish.

A record October crowd of 131,500 turned out to see Sunday's dazzling display of speed and a runaway performance by a Georgian by the name of Bill Elliott. Members of the media described Elliott as having the looks of Huckleberry Finn, a Southern drawl like Gomer Pyle, and driving prowess of the Dukes of Hazzard. Elliott, only twice a winner in Winston Cup competition, drove around Benny Parsons with 50 laps to go and stretched his lead to 14.5 seconds when the checkered flag fell.

"Benny was only a half straightaway from lapping me midway in the race," said Elliott. "Luckily, we got a caution flag and we caught up. Then it got cloudy and that helped bring the track to our set-up."

Only three cautions interrupted the brisk pace and Elliott averaged an event record 148.861 miles per hour. Cale Yarborough finished third with title contenders Gant and Labonte filling out the top five. Labonte went on to wrap up the Winston Cup championship by a 65-point margin over Gant.

By the end of the 1984 NASCAR season, Bill Elliott had hit his stride, and the momentum was to carry over into the 1985 Winston Cup campaign.

CHAPTER 11

All-Stars and the Pass in the Grass

1985-1987

Accenting the meteoric growth of NASCAR's Winston Cup Series, the 1985 season had a few new sparkling nuggets tossed into the annual calendar. The Winston Million dollar bonus posted by R.J. Reynolds was available to any driver who could pull off the unlikely feat of winning three of the four crown jewel events—the Daytona 500, Talladega's Winston 500, Charlotte's Motor Speedway's Coca-Cola World 600, and Darlington's fabled Southern 500. Only twice in the previous 16 years had a driver won three of the four majors, LeeRoy Yarbrough in 1969 and David Pearson in 1976.

Additionally, an All-Star race, coined The Winston, would be inserted into the May speedweeks program at Charlotte. The 70-lap, 105-mile event featured race winners during the 1984 season. Posted awards of a half-million bucks, with $200,000 going to the winner, would await the All-Star cast.

Darrell Waltrip (No. 11) and Bill Elliott (No. 9), principals in the 1985 NASCAR Winston Cup title chase, shared the spotlight during the May Speedweek at Charlotte. Waltrip won two of the high-profile events over Memorial Day weekend, prevailing in the inaugural The Winston All-Star race and the Coca-Cola World 600. *CMS photo by E. Lee Roane*

By 1985, Elliott and the Melling team, still stocked with family members and close friends, clawed its way into the upper echelon of NASCAR's unique game of noise and revelry.

Elliott was tall, raw-boned, and quiet, and he proved he had the courage to match his skill. He dominated the 1985 Daytona 500 to tuck away the first golden link in the Winston Million. He won the spring events at Atlanta and Darlington, and authored a miraculous comeback to win at Talladega, overcoming a 5-mile deficit without the aid of a caution flag. By winning at Talladega, he plucked the second jewel in his quest to win the Winston Million.

Elliott won again at Dover, and by the time the tour hit Charlotte, a fever pitch of alarming proportions was clearly evident. Elliott had won half the races through mid-May. He won the pole for the Coca-Cola World 600 with a four-lap average qualifying speed of 164.703 miles per hour.

A crowd of 133,200 showed up to watch Saturday's double-header, featuring the Winn-Dixie 300 NASCAR Late Model Sportsman race and The Winston. Tim Richmond, driving a Hendrick Motorsports Pontiac, led 150 of the 200 laps and easily outdistanced Neil Bonnett by 2.44 seconds to win the 300-miler.

Starting positions for the inaugural driving of The Winston were determined by the number of victories in 1984, with the pole reserved for Winston Cup champion Terry Labonte. The remainder of the dashing dozen were Darrell Waltrip, Harry Gant, Elliott, Geoff

Bosco Lowe's Oldsmobile erupts into flames following a 16th-lap crash in the 1985 Winn-Dixie 300. Lowe lost control out of the fourth turn, cut through the infield grass, and drifted into the high speed groove, where he was clobbered by Robert Ingram, Jr. Lowe bailed out of the car unharmed. *CMS photo by Don Hunter*

Lean, lanky, and fair-haired Bill Elliott and his homespun family operation trudged out of the Georgia hills in 1976 devoid of all publicity, having the unlikely vision of succeeding in NASCAR's high-energy domain. Fighting impossible odds with meager funds, the team struggled mightily during its formative years. But in 1982, entrepreneur Harry Melling purchased the team, providing proper funding and the tools that allowed Elliott to rub elbows with the established stars.

Tim Richmond and his mother, Evelyn, savor the fruits of Victory Lane following the 1985 Winn-Dixie 300 at Charlotte Motor Speedway. Richmond drove a Hendrick Motorsports Pontiac to an overwhelming victory, leading all but 39 of the 200 laps. The following season, Richmond became a full-time member of the Hendrick Motorsports operation on the NASCAR Winston Cup tour. *CMS photo by Don Hunter*

Bodine, Cale Yarborough, Dale Earnhardt, Bobby Allison, Richard Petty, Ricky Rudd, Tim Richmond, and Benny Parsons.

Waltrip bolted from the outside front row starting spot to lead the first 19 laps. He and Labonte traded the lead three times before mandatory pit stops between the 30th and 40th lap came into play. After all pit stops had been completed, Gant held a 2.7-second advantage over Labonte with Waltrip third, 3.3 seconds back.

Waltrip shot past Labonte to move into second and gradually reeled in the leader. Coming up for the white flag, Waltrip dashed past Gant to take the lead. He flashed under the checkered flag a car length in front of Gant to snare the $200,000 first prize.

The engine in Waltrip's Junior Johnson Chevrolet blew up as he was crossing the finish line. "It literally exploded," Waltrip said during post-race celebrations. "We knew we'd built one not long on duration, but we sure didn't intend to cut it that close." Elliott was not a factor and came home seventh.

A huge throng of 155,000, which oozed well beyond capacity, passed through the turnstiles for the 27th annual Coca-Cola World 600. Elliott led the first 13 laps from the pole, but faded from the hunt, victimized by a faulty radio, a flat tire, and brake failure. He eventually finished 18th, 21 laps off the pace.

The final stages of the 600 came down to a Waltrip-Gant duel for the second day in a row. Gant had taken first place in the 328th lap following a caution flag, but had to make a quick stop for fuel with 10 laps remaining. Waltrip stayed on the track and cruised into the lead.

Risking running out of fuel, Waltrip tempered his pace and managed to run the final 109.5 miles on a single tank of fuel. He drove across the finish line 14.64 seconds ahead of Gant to score his third 600 win. "The tank was bone dry when we finished the race," said Waltrip, who collected $290,733 for his back-to-back victories. "I made it because I drafted Harry a long ways before he stopped, then I drafted [Bobby] Allison at the end. Junior told me over the radio that we could make it if I drafted everything that moved." For Waltrip, it was his first win of the 1985 season, and it placed him in contention for a third Winston Cup title.

Elliott continued his rampage throughout the summer, sweeping both races at Pocono and Michigan, and winning the Winston Million at Darlington with a come-from-behind victory. He left Darlington with a 206-point bulge in the standings and appeared a shoo-in for the 1985 championship.

But in the four races between Darlington and Charlotte's Miller High Life 500, Elliott's lead had evaporated and Waltrip held a 30-point cushion as the teams geared up for the October speed fling.

The 13th annual event for NASCAR Late Model Sportsman cars had been increased to 400 laps. Terry Labonte, driving a Pontiac owned by Waltrip, led the final 51 laps and beat Geoff Bodine, Rusty Wallace, and Dale Earnhardt.

Cale Yarborough, shackled by a run of sour luck throughout the 1985 season, won the Miller High Life 500 in a formidable display of perseverance and determination. On five separate occasions, he made up a lost lap. The muscular veteran rallied sharply in the closing laps and prevailed in the vicious, hard-fought 500-mile sojourn. Many observers said it was one of the most exceptional drives in a career filled with remarkable accomplishments. "I had a flat tire, got outrun, ran out of gas—and it was a real fight to keep coming back," said Yarborough after his third win in the autumn classic.

Yarborough wasn't overly large of build, but he was made of granite, with a thick neck and tremendous

spirit—and he had to rely on all of his attributes to come out on top in the 500.

Waltrip went on to earn his third NASCAR Winston Cup championship, finishing 101 points ahead of 11-time winner Bill Elliott in the final tally.

In 1986, sanctioning NASCAR adopted new series titles for the top two stock car racing divisions. What was officially known as the Winston Cup Grand National tour since 1971 simply became Winston Cup in 1986. The Grand National tag, which had been affiliated with NASCAR's top series since 1950, was assigned to the Busch Grand National Series, previously known as the Late Model Sportsman division.

Dale Earnhardt and Geoff Bodine grabbed most of the early season headlines in 1986, each having won twice by the time the tour arrived at Charlotte Motor Speedway for the 27th annual Coca-Cola 600. Bodine and Hendrick Motorsports teammate Tim Richmond qualified on the front row, with Earnhardt third.

During Friday's practice session, Richard Petty's Pontiac snapped a suspension part and clobbered the retaining wall. The car was demolished and King

Teammates Tim Richmond and Geoff Bodine occupy the front row for the 1986 Oakwood Homes 500. Richmond, in his first season with Hendrick Motorsports, had won 6 of the previous 13 Winston Cup events. After starting in third position, Dale Earnhardt motored to victory in the 500-miler. The skeleton of the elaborate Smith Tower, in its early stages of construction, rises above the front stretch grandstands. *CMS Archives*

Freshman driver Alan Kulwicki pits his No. 35 Quincy's Steak House Ford during the 1986 Oakwood Homes 500. As a rookie, Kulwicki assumed ownership of the team from Bill Terry midway through the season, maintained his stride, and won the Rookie of the Year award. The Wisconsin driver had little more than a rag tag crew and only one car for most of the campaign. He affectionately nicknamed the sturdy car "sirloin" because of its toughness. Kulwicki scored 4 top-10 finishes in the 23 starts of his rookie season. *CMS Archives*

Richard was knocked unconscious. In a curious and unexplained decision by sanctioning NASCAR, Petty was not permitted to bring in a back-up car for the 600 although two back-up cars competed in the Daytona 500 in February. Forced to withdraw his car, Petty was able to pick up a ride in D.K. Ulrich's Chevrolet, which had been qualified by Trevor Boys. Petty placed some STP decals on the green-and-white Chevrolet No. 6 and started in 37th place.

Tim Richmond annihilated the field in the ninth annual Winn-Dixie 300, finishing in a lap by himself. Brett Bodine and Davey Allison ran second and third, respectively, before a crowd of 91,600.

In Sunday's Coca-Cola 600, Cale Yarborough and Tim Richmond ruled the roost in the early going as Earnhardt faded back in the pack. After 400 miles, Earnhardt was in danger of going a lap down to leader Cale Yarborough, but a caution brought on by a rain shower drew him back into the hunt.

"When Cale was coming up to lap me, all I could see was those hamburger eyes of his," said Earnhardt. "I was able to hold him off until the caution came out. Holding off Cale was my last shot. If he'd have lapped me, I'd have been blown out of the water."

Given new life, Earnhardt became a factor. Although he never led until the 327th lap, he cruised to a 1.9-second triumph over Tim Richmond as Yarborough fell to third.

Earnhardt had been atop the Winston Cup point standings since April and brought a 122-point lead to Charlotte when teams began gearing up for October's Oakwood Homes 500. Earnhardt was an uncompromising competitor on NASCAR's golden high banks. His intensity in the face of competition was written on his face, as if riveted by steel.

Earnhardt led 194 of the 200 laps in winning the All Pro Auto Parts 300 for NASCAR Busch Grand National cars, thoroughly beating a diverse field.

Luck seemed to abandon Earnhardt in the early laps of the Oakwood Homes 500. A pair of green flag pit stops to replace cut tires dropped him two laps off the pace. When he returned to full song, he was barely in the top 30. Making use of timely caution flags and the cunningness of his driving, Earnhardt made up both laps in a 30-mile span. Once back in contention, he breezed to an easy victory over Harry Gant.

Earnhardt captured the 1986 Winston Cup championship by a comfortable 288-point margin over Darrell Waltrip. In 1987 he picked up where he left off, winning six of the first eight races, establishing a new record for near-perfection at the outset of a campaign. Earnhardt combined great stamina, a cool head, mental alertness,

and superior ability to become the brightest star in NASCAR's constellation.

By May of 1987, the Smith Tower, a 12-story, 100,000 square-foot steel and glass specimen of architectural excellence, opened to the public, albeit in incomplete form. The Speedway Club, a private club offering members world-class, year-round dining and entertainment, occupied the top two floors of the structure. When completed, the building contained privately leased office space, a souvenir store, and the Charlotte Motor Speedway corporate offices.

"Auto racing is only as good as the host facility," said chairman of the board Bruton Smith. "The Speedway Club is the supreme testament to our belief in the future of racing at Charlotte Motor Speedway. We have spared no expense to guarantee the absolute best in entertainment, dining, and amenities. There isn't a finer, more elegant entertainment setting in the South."

The third running of The Winston returned to Charlotte Motor Speedway in 1987 following a one-year hiatus to Atlanta. The format for the All-Star event had been massaged to include the 19 most-recent winners in Winston Cup competition along with the victor of the preliminary Winston Open. The race was also broken down into three segments: 70 laps, a 50-lapper, and a 10-lap shootout.

Among the 19 entrants was Tim Richmond, a flashy, gifted chauffeur who won seven races in 1986, then was physically unable to meet the opening bell in 1987. Although originally believed to be suffering from a case of double pneumonia, Richmond was actually enduring the devastating effects of AIDS.

Geoff Bodine's Chevrolet lurches sideways at the start of the final 10-lap dash in the 1987 The Winston. As Bodine looped his car and Bill Elliott checked up, Dale Earnhardt shot into the lead. By using the now famous "pass in the grass," Earnhardt prevailed in the third-annual running of the NASCAR All-Star race. *CMS Archives*

Bitter rivals Geoff Bodine and Dale Earnhardt, two principal figures in The Winston, clash again in the closing laps of the Winn-Dixie 300 NASCAR Busch Grand National event. The incident took both drivers out of contention, and Harry Gant scampered home first. *CMS Archives*

After a brief caution, the green flashed on with Earnhardt and Elliott battling like a couple of pit bulls. Coming off turn four with five laps to go, Elliott got the nose of his Ford under Earnhardt's Chevrolet. Earnhardt steered his car to the left to make the block—but the two cars touched. Earnhardt went skittering through the grass and miraculously, came back onto the track still in the lead. Inflamed to a fever pitch, Earnhardt had been the architect of what was to become known as "the pass in the grass."

Elliott mustered one final attempt to regain the lead, pulling along the high side of Earnhardt in turn four. Earnhardt rode Elliott toward the wall, forcing him to lift. Two laps later, Elliott blew a tire and was out of contention. Earnhardt went on to win, with Terry Labonte finishing second and Richmond third. Bodine came back to finish fourth while Elliott was credited with a 14th-place finish.

Motorsports journalist Benny Phillips declared that the ending needed "a few bars from the William Tell Overture" and "a background voice which once introduced the Lone Ranger radio show, 'And now from those thrilling days of yesteryear, we bring you The Winston.'

"For it was out of the past and it was show," continued Phillips. "It was entertainment of the highest order. It lulled you to sleep until the final 10 laps, then wham, bam, thank you ma'am and all hell broke loose just as you would expect for $200,000. Jesse James stopped at nothing when he robbed a big bank."

After the race, Elliott popped Earnhardt on the cool-off lap. Bodine weaved his way through traffic with reckless abandon but did not strike anybody. Elliott was livid afterwards. "If a man has to put you out, it ain't right," Elliott said after climbing out of his car. "He pulled over and let me get beside him, then drove me into the wall. I'd say that was done deliberately."

Astonishingly, he crawled off his death bed to compete in The Winston.

Starting from the pole, Bill Elliott made a mockery of the opening two segments, leading all but four of the 125 laps. He started on the pole for the final dash with Geoff Bodine flanking him on the outside and Earnhardt tucked on the tail of Bodine.

Bodine got the jump on Elliott at the start. As the cars raced into the first turn, Elliott was pinched onto the apron. Contact was made between Elliott and Bodine that left Bodine spinning. Earnhardt shot under both rivals into the lead.

Earnhardt was willing to point fingers in the other direction. "Elliott clipped me and turned me sideways. I guarantee if I had turned someone sideways like that, I'd be hanging from the flagpole right now. He waited on me after the race and tried to run me into the wall," declared the winner.

Earnhardt, Elliott, and Bodine were all fined by NASCAR and told to cool down for the Coca-Cola 600.

Third-generation driver Kyle Petty, manning the Wood Brothers Ford, outlasted the competition and produced an upset victory in the 1987 Coca-Cola 600. It was the Wood Brothers' fourth triumph in the 600 and sixth at Charlotte. For Petty, it was his first win on a superspeedway. *CMS Archives*

Harry Gant clawed his way to victory in the Winn-Dixie 300 on Saturday, but his triumph was overshadowed by another Earnhardt-Bodine bumping session. With 13 laps to go, Bodine nipped the bumper of Earnhardt, who got sideways but wrestled his car back under control. Bodine was hit by Larry Pearson and all combatants were out of contention.

Third-generation driver Kyle Petty won the 28th running of the Coca-Cola 600 before a record audience of 165,000. Driving the Wood Brothers Ford, Petty survived a day of attrition as only 17 cars in the field of 42 were running at the finish. Morgan Shepherd finished second, more than a lap behind. Rusty Wallace was leading until 17 laps to go when a sputtering engine knocked him off the pace. He eventually wound up 10th, four laps behind.

Earnhardt had problems from the outset and limped home 20th, 95 laps off the pace. Elliott went out while leading in the 267th lap and Bodine encountered numerous problems and wound up 18th. There were no additional on-track fireworks between the heated rivals.

By October, the 1987 Winston Cup championship chase was history. Earnhardt carried a 573-point cushion into the Oakwood Homes 500 and there was virtually no hope of anyone catching him.

Bobby Allison put his Stavola Brothers Buick on the pole with a speed of 171.636 miles per hour, the first pole he had earned since 1982.

The 15th annual All Pro 300 for NASCAR Busch Grand National cars consisted of a two-part format. After 101 laps had been run, there was a 15-minute intermission during which pit crews could dial the cars in. The remaining 99 laps were run following a two-abreast restart. The format drew mixed reactions from contestants and fans alike. Harry Gant held off Darrell Waltrip in a stirring finish to notch the victory.

Sunday's Oakwood Homes 500 was a tortuous affair with no fewer than 11 cars being eliminated by wrecks. Many others were running at reduced speed with mangled bodywork. Neil Bonnett was seriously injured on the 58th lap when his Pontiac blew a tire and slammed into the fourth turn wall. It took rescue workers over 20 minutes to remove him from the car. Bonnett suffered a broken hip in the accident and would be out for the season.

Bill Elliott dodged the multitude of wrecks and finished 2.22 seconds in front of Allison to score his second win at Charlotte Motor Speedway.

Earnhardt coasted to the 1987 NASCAR Winston Cup title by a 489-point margin over Bill Elliott. He became only the fifth driver to win three championships.

Dale Earnhardt (No. 3), Buddy Baker (No. 88), and Geoff Bodine (No. 5) hook up in a classic three-abreast formation in the early stages of the 1987 Coca-Cola 600. Baker wheeled his Oldsmobile to 7th place finish while Bodine and Earnhardt ran into an assortment of problems and finished 18th and 20th, respectively. *CMS Archives*

Bill Elliott is joined by Bruton Smith in Victory Lane after the 1987 Oakwood Homes 500. It was Elliott's second win at Charlotte Motor Speedway and the 20th of his career. Elliott never led the race until the 273rd lap, but from that point on he was never headed and cruised to an easy victory. *CMS photo by Don Hunter*

CHARLOTTE MOTO

CHAPTER 12

Clash of the Titans

1988–1990

The 1988 NASCAR Winston Cup season acquired kaleidoscopic characteristics early in the campaign. With upstart Hoosier Tire Company vying for a foothold in the sport against corporate giant Goodyear, the race results often looked like enhanced typographical errors.

The first nine Winston Cup events on the 1988 slate produced seven different winners, including unlikely Victory Lane participants Lake Speed and Phil Parsons. Speed prevailed at Darlington on Hoosier tires for his first big-league triumph and Parsons shellacked the field at Talladega with a nifty display of speed and endurance. It was the first time Victory Lane had been graced with two new smiling faces in the season's first nine races since 1970.

Terry Labonte, seemingly out of the hunt midway through the 1989 The Winston, made up a lap and stormed to victory in the final 10-lap segment to post a popular win in the fifth-annual NASCAR All-Star race. Labonte had fallen a lap off the pace due to a cut tire but scrambled back into contention in the closing laps. He made a dash from sixth place to the lead in a lap and a half and led the final nine laps to pocket the $200,000 winner's prize. *CMS photo by Don Hunter*

The fourth running of The Winston at Charlotte Motor Speedway on May 22, 1988, featured the 19 most recent Winston Cup race winners and Sterling Marlin, who won the Winston Open. Marlin, driving Billy Hagan's Oldsmobile, edged Alan Kulwicki by an eyelash at the finish of the 100-lap preliminary event.

Darrell Waltrip led the opening 32 laps of the first 75-lap segment from the pole. Sophomore sensation Davey Allison and three-time NASCAR champion Dale Earnhardt then took center stage, with Allison nosing out Earnhardt at the finish. As Earnhardt backed off, the right front tire blew, sending him into the wall in the first turn. For all intents and purposes, his run for the $200,000 first prize was over, although he was able to continue in the other two segments at reduced speed.

Bill Elliott won the middle segment, a 50-lap dash that was interrupted when Ricky Rudd popped a tire on his Buick and crashed hard in the second turn. Rudd tore a knee ligament in the crash.

Terry Labonte, who had fallen a lap off the pace early when a tire blistered, managed to get back into

The lengthy feud between Dale Earnhardt and Geoff Bodine continued in the 1988 Coca-Cola 600. Earnhardt's No. 3 Chevrolet and Bodine's car got together early in the event, sending Bodine into a spin. In a controversial and much-discussed decision, NASCAR officials set Earnhardt down five laps, effectively removing him from contention. *CMS Archives*

Alan Kulwicki is hoisted tall in the pole-cat chair after setting a new track record for the 1988 Oakwood Homes 500. The popular Kulwicki shattered the previous mark by more than 4 mph in a stunning performance, and his new qualifying speed of 175.896 mph stood for another three years. *CMS Archives*

Youthful exuberance prevailed over old age and treachery in the 1989 Champion Spark Plug 300 Busch Grand National race. Twenty-one-year-old Rob Moroso took advantage of Rusty Wallace's late race ill-fortune, rode into the lead six laps from the finish, and outran Darrell Waltrip in a stirring final-lap duel. *CMS Archives*

the lead lap following a timely caution flag. Starting sixth in the final 10-lap dash, Labonte put the spurs to his Junior Johnson Chevrolet, passed five cars in the first lap and breezed into the lead a lap later. Texas Terry held off Sterling Marlin by less than a second at the finish. Davey Allison, Elliott, and Bobby Allison rounded out the top five.

The alarming number of blistered and blown tires in The Winston caused concerns in the Goodyear camp. Five days before the 29th annual Coca-Cola 600, Goodyear pulled its tires out of the garage area, leaving all cars on Hoosiers except Dave Marcis, who went against company wishes and mounted Goodyears anyway.

The Winn-Dixie 300 NASCAR Busch Grand National race was run in two 100-lap segments, which was more of a safety net for Dale Jarrett than a dandy promotional item. In the final laps of the first segment, Jarrett's Oldsmobile broke a rocker arm, knocking him well off the pace. During the 15-minute intermission, Jarrett's crew was able to replace the faulty part and he barely made the green flag restart.

In the 117th lap, Dale Earnhardt and Geoff Bodine, raw rivals personified, renewed their bumper-to-bumper theatrics before a crowd of 94,500. Earnhardt's Chevrolet nipped Bodine's rear bumper, spinning him down the backstretch. "I don't know what happened. I wasn't watching. I was out front. I must have hit an oil slick," Bodine said, with tongue firmly planted in cheek.

Predictably, Earnhardt had a different version. "Bodine came down and pinched me off. I bumped him and turned him around. That's racin', ain't it?" he declared whimsically. While NASCAR had increased the roll call in its penalty box in recent months, neither Bodine nor Earnhardt was reprimanded in the 300.

Jarrett came from fifth to first in the final nine laps of the 300-miler to claim his first win on a superspeedway. He nosed out Bobby Hillin, Jr., and Bobby Allison at the finish.

Sunday's Coca-Cola 600 was a brutal affair. Tires blew with stunning regularity. Harry Gant broke a leg in two places following a crash near the midpoint of the race. Neil Bonnett suffered shoulder and knee injuries when he blew a tire and crashed. Buddy Baker was knocked woozy in a multi-car accident on lap 244. While Baker was initially given a clean bill of health, his injuries proved far more serious than first thought. A blood clot formed on his brain and he was forced into semi-retirement later in the summer.

Team owner Bud Moore was run over on pit road by his driver, Brett Bodine, breaking his leg. Dave

Darrell Waltrip's Chevrolet breaks loose in the fourth turn after a tap from Rusty Wallace in the 1989 The Winston. The incident occurred with just over a lap remaining as Waltrip held a narrow lead. Wallace went on to win and Waltrip slid to ninth. Ironically, Waltrip, once the subject of jeers from the trackside audience, became a darling of the racing fans and won the 1989 Most Popular Driver award. Wallace, who had the adulation of the spectators for nearly 10 years, became the recipient of unfavorable reaction during drivers' introductions for over a year. *CMS Archives*

Dale Jarrett (No. 32) edges Dick Trickle by less than 3 feet at the finish of the 1990 Champion Spark Plug 300 in perhaps the closest finish in the history of the Speedway. Trickle had led for 33 laps, but Jarrett squeezed past in the final lap. Third-place finisher Harry Gant is only a car length behind. *CMS Archives*

Charlotte Motor Speedway, once tagged a "white elephant" as it struggled during its early years, had become the most modern automobile racing plant in the country by 1989. Parking lots are jammed, every seat is occupied, and virtually every available space in the infield is filled. *CMS Archives*

Marcis miraculously walked away from a savage wreck. In all, there were 13 caution flags for 89 laps.

Punctuating the hair-raising event was the resurgence of the Earnhardt-Bodine squabble. Early in the race, Earnhardt and Bodine got together and Bodine took a trip into the wall. NASCAR officials set Earnhardt down in the penalty box for five laps, effectively removing him from the hunt.

Darrell Waltrip carefully steered around the carnage and scored his fourth win in the 600 and his fifth at Charlotte Motor Speedway. When the 4-hour, 49-minute spectacle mercifully ended, Waltrip had averaged only 124.460 miles per hour and had become the eighth different winner in the first 10 races of 1988.

By October, 13 different drivers had won Winston Cup events, and Bill Elliott had managed to build a 124-point lead in the championship standings. Bobby Allison, who was recovering from life-threatening injuries suffered at Pocono in June, was absent from the active roster after the accident.

One of the young stars on the horizon expected to make a rapid ascent into NASCAR's major leagues was Rob Moroso, who celebrated his 20th birthday the week before the 16th annual All Pro Auto Parts 300 Busch Series race. Moroso qualified 13th on the grid but crashed in practice on Friday. Saturday morning he missed the driver's meeting while assisting the crew in repairing the car. Forced to start 41st, Moroso delivered

a most memorable performance. Possessing unusual athletic skills blended nicely with a fierce competitive spirit, Moroso rallied to take the lead late in the race. He held off Geoff Bodine and Bobby Hillin, Jr., to win in a stirring finish.

"This is great," shouted the boyish winner. "It makes me dizzy. I wasn't sure if I could hold off Geoff until the last lap. When he didn't get by me in the laps before the white flag, I knew he wasn't going to on the last lap."

Moroso made his Winston Cup debut in the 29th annual Oakwood Homes 500. He did a creditable job, finishing 14th.

Rusty Wallace started third in the 500, behind pole-sitter Alan Kulwicki and Bill Elliott. He flexed his muscles early but had to make three pit stops between laps 112 and 142 for a skip in the engine. Losing two laps in the process, Wallace was considered out of contention.

"The engine developed a bad miss and we never did figure out what it was," Wallace said later. "We were running on seven-and-a-half cylinders the rest of the way."

Despite the overwhelming deficit and a steed that didn't fully respond to his command, Wallace authored a comeback for the ages. In the 222nd lap, he buzzed past leader Bobby Hillin, Jr., to make up a lap. On lap 285, he scooted back into the lead lap. From that point Wallace chased down the leaders and assumed command with 12 laps remaining. With Darrell Waltrip hot on his heels, Wallace blocked every attempt and came home the winner by a car length. The crowd, estimated at 145,000, was on its collective feet the final 50 miles.

Wallace rallied sharply in the final five races of the 1988 season, winning four of them, but still fell 24 points shy of catching Elliott in the chase for the Winston Cup title.

Wallace and Waltrip supplied the fireworks in the fifth annual running of The Winston at Charlotte Motor Speedway in 1989. The carnival of courage and another chapter in the clash of the titans was played at center stage before 84,637 spectators in the All-Star event.

The two heated rivals shared victory in the 75- and 50-lap opening segments, and both started on the front row for the heart-thumping 10-lap dash for cash. Waltrip breezed to an early lead, but Wallace was able to apply pressure in the waning laps. Coming off the fourth turn as the pair approached the white flag, Wallace's Pontiac flicked the rear bumper of Waltrip's Chevrolet, sending the three-time NASCAR champion sliding into the grass.

Wallace held his position at the front for the final lap restart and hustled to a three-car-length triumph over Ken Schrader. Wallace won $240,000, while Waltrip got $55,000 for finishing seventh.

"It was an ugly win," said a steamed Waltrip. "He drove into me and spun me out. It was pretty flagrant. I hope he chokes on that $200,000."

Wallace used the well-worn and easily applicable phrase "that's racing. I think every driver who starts The Winston, including myself, had better be ready for some paint changing. If they are out for a gentleman drive on Sunday, then they don't need to be in this race. It's a tough race designed to show who the best of the best is."

Wallace received a chorus of boos from many in the grandstands. "I feel uneasy right now," Wallace continued. "I'm happy I won, but the fans who are booing me is what's bugging me the most."

In Saturday's Champion Filter 300 Busch Grand National event, Rob Moroso scored a victory nearly

Mark Martin (No. 6) leads Morgan Shepherd (No. 15) and a thundering herd into the first turn during the opening laps of the 1990 The Winston. While Dale Earnhardt made a runaway of the All-Star contest, a furious battle raged on for runner-up honors. Ken Schrader came from ninth to grab second place in the closing laps. *CMS photo by David Chobat*

Dale Earnhardt became the first driver to lead flag-to-flag in the 1990 The Winston. Earnhardt, an enduring enigma in the motorsports world, started on the pole in the familiar GM Goodwrench Chevrolet and led all 105 miles in a dominating performance. *CMS Archives*

Davey Allison ducks inside Ernie Irvan during the 1990 Mello Yello 500. Allison was mired in a slump most of the 1990 NASCAR Winston Cup season, having won only one short-track event before the Charlotte race. Allison grabbed the lead with just 12 laps remaining and drove the Robert Yates Ford to his first of two victories at Charlotte. *Bryan Hallman*

In 1990, Rusty Wallace was in his fifth and final year driving for drag racing icon Raymond Beadle. The defending NASCAR Winston Cup champion failed to make a viable bid for a second title in a row, but he did win two races, including the Coca-Cola 600. Wallace led the final 91 laps in a dazzling display of prowess in the 600-miler. *Bryan Hallman*

identical to his win in October of 1988. The Connecticut youngster dropped a lap off the pace, motored back into contention, and took the lead for good with seven laps remaining when leader Rusty Wallace developed engine problems. Moroso held runner-up Darrell Waltrip at bay in the final laps and scored his second straight victory at Charlotte Motor Speedway.

The anticipated rematch between Waltrip and Wallace in the 30th edition of the Coca-Cola 600 never developed. Wallace ran well and led 22 laps, but retired with a blown engine. Waltrip led the final 80 trips around the Charlotte Motor Speedway and came home a winner in the 600 for a record fifth time.

"It's a fitting end for a difficult week," said Waltrip. "What happened in The Winston lit a fire under me and my crew guys that no extinguisher could put out. We felt if we ran all 600 miles we'd be in Victory Lane, and that's the way it turned out."

By October the chase for the NASCAR Winston Cup championship had been whittled to two combatants, point leader Dale Earnhardt and Wallace, who trailed by 75 points. Wallace qualified sixth for the All Pro Auto Parts 500 with Earnhardt turning in the 12th-quickest speed. Bill Elliott won the pole at 174.081 miles per hour.

Twenty-two-year-old Rob Moroso sped to victory in Saturday's All Pro 300 NASCAR Busch Grand National event, taking the lead for keeps with 28 laps to go. Michael Waltrip finished a close second. For Moroso, it was his third straight 300-mile triumph at Charlotte Motor Speedway.

Sunday's 500-miler changed the landscape of the 1989 championship chase. Earnhardt wheeled his Goodwrench Chevrolet into the garage area on the 13th lap with a broken camshaft. He was out of the running and locked in 42nd finishing position. It opened the door for Wallace to make a run for the point lead.

Wallace led for a 45-lap stretch early, then ran comfortably just behind the leaders. Mark Martin, still seeking his first Winston Cup victory, gradually pulled away from the field toward the end of the race. While holding an 11-second lead, Martin peeled into the pits for his final pit stop on lap 295 of the 334-lap contest. His Roush Racing crew changed four tires and he returned to the track trailing Ken Schrader.

Schrader made his last pit stop on lap 310, taking on two right-side tires. When Schrader returned to the track in full song, he trailed Martin by only 3.0 seconds. With four fresh tires, Martin was expected to pull away with ease. But one of those four tires was losing air. Schrader buzzed past Martin with 15 laps to go and breezed to an uncontested victory. Harry Gant got by Martin with a handful of laps remaining and took second. Martin held on for third. Wallace finished seventh and took a 35-point lead in the Winston Cup standings.

"I'm big-time disappointed," Martin reflected moments after the race. "We had the field skinned. It's a hard pill to swallow. This race was ours until we had the tire problems."

After a near miss in the 1988 championship chase, Rusty Wallace edged Earnhardt by 12 points to capture the 1989 Winston Cup title.

The sixth edition of The Winston All-Star race, staged on May 20, 1990, was reduced to a 70-lap

affair: a 50-lap opening segment followed by a 20-lap dash. Dale Earnhardt won the pole and led all the way in a dominating performance that was devoid of the usual fireworks.

"This is the kind of race I wanted to run and win today," said Earnhardt, who became the first two-time winner of the All-Star contest. "No controversy, no rifts."

Dale Jarrett squeezed past Dick Trickle in the final lap to win the Champion 300 NASCAR Busch Grand National race. Trickle led 114 of the 200 laps around Charlotte's mile-and-a-half but bobbled briefly in the fourth turn of the final lap. Jarrett poked the nose of his Pontiac under Trickle and won the race to the finish line by 3 feet. It was the only lap Jarrett led all afternoon.

A crowd of nearly 150,000 turned out to watch the 31st annual running of the Coca-Cola 600. The huge throng watched Rusty Wallace lead 306 of the 400 laps and cruise to an uneventful triumph. Bill Elliott wound up second with Mark Martin third.

Dale Earnhardt entered the race with a 90-point lead in the Winston Cup standings but blew a tire and crashed on lap 150. His Richard Childress crew made repairs and Earnhardt managed to finish 30th. He left Charlotte with a 21-point lead in his quest to win a fourth Winston Cup title.

By October, Earnhardt and Mark Martin were locked in a tight battle in the championship chase. Martin had led the Winston Cup standings since June but Earnhardt was on the prowl and only trailed by 16 points entering Charlotte's Motor Speedway's Mello Yello 500.

Tuning up for Sunday's 500, Earnhardt and Martin both competed in the All Pro Auto Parts 300 on Saturday. Sterling Marlin, who started 32nd on the grid, charged past Greg Sacks with six laps remaining to snare his first Busch Grand National victory. Sacks finished second with Dale Jarrett third and Earnhardt fourth. Mark Martin wound up 16th, a lap off the pace.

Neither Earnhardt nor Martin was a factor in the Mello Yello 500. Neither led a lap and both finished miles behind winner Davey Allison. Bill Elliott led 243 of the first 258 laps, but his dominant ride was interrupted by three unscheduled pit stops. A brake caliper broke on his Melling Racing Ford, which generated heat and caused a tire to repeatedly deflate. Elliott wound up 15th—just behind Martin, who struggled on seven cylinders most of the day.

Earnhardt was foiled by a pit road collision with Ernie Irvan, a spinout, and a costly pit miscue. Earnhardt peeled out of the pits without the left-side tires securely in place, and when he got to the first turn, they popped off. The RCR Enterprises crew rushed to Earnhardt's disabled car, replaced the tires, and got him back in the race. Earnhardt finished 25th and fell 49 points behind Martin in the Winston Cup standings.

Despite the setback, Earnhardt rallied in the final three races of the 1990 season and won his fourth NASCAR championship by a slim 26-point margin.

Darrell Waltrip missed nine races in the 1990 Winston Cup season after he was injured in a practice crash at Daytona in July. Still walking with the aid of crutches in October, Waltrip gingerly climbed into his Chevrolet and drove to an impressive ninth-place finish in the Mello Yello 500. *Brian Czobat*

Mark Martin and team owner Jack Roush entered the 1990 Mello Yello 500 with a 16-point lead in the Winston Cup standings. Martin's closest adversary, Dale Earnhardt, endured a terrible day, finishing 25th. But Martin was unable to capitalize on Earnhardt's misfortune and came home 14th in the final order. While Martin did extend his lead to 49 points, Earnhardt rallied in the final three races and took the championship by 26 points over Martin. *CMS photo by David Chobat*

CHAPTER 13

Sizzling Days and One Hot Night

1991–1993

A tantalizing and mind-teasing event was added to the 1991 Winston All-Star weekend on May 18 and 19. T. Wayne Robertson, senior vice president of sports marketing for sponsoring R.J. Reynolds Tobacco Company, arranged a special race for retired Winston Cup icons. "For several years we have wanted to present the pioneers to today's fans in a way that would be enjoyed by everyone," said Robertson. "We're celebrating our 20th year in the sport and decided that The Winston weekend would be a good time to do it."

Robertson conceived the idea and fostered it into a reality. Twenty-two former drivers from NASCAR's most colorful era would race full-bodied stock cars around the flat quarter-mile oval situated along the front stretch of the Charlotte Motor Speedway. Two dozen identically prepared cars were groomed by part-time campaigner Rodney Combs. Twenty-two cars with livery once made famous by the high-octane drivers themselves were ready for what turned out to be a 30-lap slugfest.

Rusty Wallace (No. 2) ducks under Greg Sacks during the 1993 Coca-Cola 600. Wallace had his best season in 1993, winning 10 NASCAR Winston Cup events. Wallace won the most races, recorded more top-5 and top-10 finishes than any other driver, and led more laps during the course of the season, but fell victim to the complexities of the point system and wound up a distant second to Dale Earnhardt. *Brian Czobat*

NASCAR's version of the Seniors Tour competed in a 30-lapper at Charlotte in 1991. In one of the most entertaining spectacles ever seen at the track, mishaps and fender benders were plentiful. Larry Frank (No. 76) and Junior Johnson skid through the turn early in the race. Elmo Langley (No. 64) started 16th in the field of 22 and won on the final lap. *CMS Archives*

Interest in the Winston Legends Shootout exceeded that of the seventh annual All-Star race, and the soldiers from a golden era of the sport were basking in the limelight. The competitors had gained a few pounds over the years, which prompted Elmo Langley to remark: "This is the first race I've ever seen where they need the Jaws of Life to get drivers into the cars, not just out of them."

The 22 mischievous drivers, each demonstrating unbridled courage, put on one whale of a show. Dick Brooks led the opening 21 laps from the pole, but a gaggle of ornery old codgers slashed their way to the front, bouncing off each other with alarming and delightful regularity.

Spins and accidents were plentiful. It took 25 minutes to complete the first 10 laps. The turns were littered with so much debris they looked like motel rooms just vacated by rock groups.

Junior Johnson carved his way into contention from his 18th starting slot, leaving a telltale residue of his white No. 3 on virtually every car he passed. He locked horns with Tim Flock on numerous occasions, three or four times under racing conditions and a couple more under the yellow flag. Junior even placed a tire burn on the side of the pace car, manned by NASCAR President Bill France, Jr. The entire spectacle was a hoot. "They told me I didn't have to bring back anything but the steering wheel," said Johnson. "There ain't much else left."

Cale Yarborough forged his way into the lead and held it until the final lap, when Langley squeezed past to take a most popular victory. Total prize money for the frolicking seniors? Nothing. But the show was worth a million bucks. Yarborough finished second with Paul Goldsmith, Neil Castles, and Fred Lorenzen rounding out the top five.

In The Winston, Davey Allison drove his Robert Yates Ford to an overwhelming triumph, leading every lap and coasting to an easy victory over Ken Schrader.

The Winston Legends Shootout, in terms of excitement, made up for the ho-hum main attraction. "Never in the three decades of racing at Charlotte Motor Speedway has there ever been anything more entertaining than the Legends race with all those graybeards," said journalist Ron Green.

With the shenanigans of the All-Star weekend aside, matters got down to serious business for Memorial Day weekend. With so much prestige and money on the line, a couple of teams hit on the magic setup and both the Champion Spark Plug 300 and the Coca-Cola 600 were routs.

Dale Earnhardt buried himself with a 19th starting position for the 300-mile NASCAR Busch Grand National event. It only took him 52 laps to thunder to the front. Once Earnhardt had the lead, he never lost it, leading the final 149 laps and finishing ahead of Dick Trickle and Harry Gant.

Mark Martin (No. 6) and Michael Waltrip (No. 30) occupy the front row for the start of the 1991 Coca-Cola 600. Martin led the first three laps but drifted from contention and eventually departed with engine problems. Waltrip led twice for nine laps and settled for a 15th-place finish. *CMS Archives*

Davey Allison and team owner Robert Yates enjoy the Victory Lane ceremonies following the 1991 The Winston. Allison led the All-Star race from start to finish and came back the following week and led 264 of the 400 laps in winning the Coca-Cola 600. *CMS photo by Don Hunter*

Bill Elliott (No. 9) slides into the infield grass after losing control of his Ford in the 1991 Coca-Cola 600. Lake Speed, in Cale Yarborough's No. 66 Pontiac, scoots by unscathed. In 1991, Elliott was in his 10th and final year with team owner Harry Melling. While the pair struck a magical chord during their tenure together, winning 34 races and the 1988 NASCAR Winston Cup title, success began to elude them in the 1990s. Elliott wound up 11th in the final 1991 points standings. The first time in nine years he had finished outside the top six. *CMS Archives*

Davey Allison and Alan Kulwicki lead the field into the first turn during the 1991 Mello Yello 500. Allison finished second in the 500-miler, which was won by Geoff Bodine. Kulwicki brought his Ford home in third place. *Brian Czobat*

In Sunday's 32nd annual Coca-Cola 600, Davey Allison galloped to an easy victory, leading 264 of the 400 laps. Giving Ford its first official win of the season, Allison led all but six of the final 94 laps and crossed under the checkered flag comfortably ahead of runner-up Ken Schrader.

By October, Earnhardt was well on his way to his fifth NASCAR Winston Cup championship, but it was Harry Gant who had captured the hearts and the imagination of the racing world. The 51-year-old veteran, riding a steed manicured by Andy Petree, had reeled off four Winston Cup victories in a row during the month of September and a couple of Busch Grand National events for good measure. Only brake failure in the final 10 laps prevented Gant from scoring his fifth-consecutive triumph at North Wilkesboro after leading for 350 of the 400 laps.

Gantmania was in full swing during Mello Yello 500 week at Charlotte Motor Speedway. Entered in both Saturday and Sunday events, Gant was the subject of both media and fan frenzy.

Curiously, Gant failed to earn a starting berth in qualifying for the 19th annual All Pro Auto Parts 300. Forced to start in the 40-lap Last Chance race, Gant wheeled Ed Whitaker's Buick to victory, earning him the 33rd starting position for the 300.

Pole-sitter Ward Burton took off at the green flag and ran away from the field as Gant scrambled through the pack. Burton proceeded to lead 162 of the first 188 laps, then with victory in sight, ran out of fuel. Gant breezed into the lead at that point and finished 13.7 seconds ahead of Ken Schrader.

Mark Martin played the part of the rabbit in Sunday's Mello Yello 500, leading for 198 of the first 211 laps when a blown engine ruined his brilliant run. Davey Allison appeared to be in the catbird seat following Martin's departure. He led 57 laps when he made his final routine pit stop for fuel on lap 317. Geoff Bodine, driving Junior Johnson's Ford, drove into the lead and as rival crews watched in disbelief, Bodine never came in for his final fuel stop. He ran the final 114 miles on one tank of fuel and coasted across the finish line well ahead of Allison to score his first win of the season.

Following the Charlotte event, Earnhardt was able to protect his point lead and went on to capture his fifth national driving championship by 195 points over Ricky Rudd.

Contracts for the annual renewal of The Winston were lingering in a lethargic state in late 1991. The two most recent runnings of the All-Star event had produced little excitement and few memorable moments. "The fate of The Winston was in doubt," admitted Charlotte Motor Speedway president Humpy Wheeler. "We proposed to light our speedway. There are 950 speedways in the United States; 850 of them run under the lights. Bruton and I both came from the short tracks. It was no small challenge to light a one-and-a-half mile superspeedway."

The contract for The Winston was renewed and Wheeler's proposal would give NASCAR Winston Cup racing its first superspeedway race run under lights since 1955.

Musco Sports Lighting, a company located in Oskaloosa, Iowa, tackled the monumental task. The lighting system cost $1.7 million and it consisted of 1,200 fixtures, 56 poles from 70 to 110 feet tall, 160 tons of steel, 1,700 mirrors, 75 miles of wire, 520 tons of concrete, and over 11 tons of glass. The system would cost about $140 per hour to operate.

Speedway chairman Bruton Smith, chairman of the board at Charlotte Motor Speedway, flipped the power switch on April 15, 1992, during a special sneak preview, and in a flash, 1.2 billion candlepower that consumed 2 million watts of power came to life. The electric evening drew 38,000 spectators, all of whom stood and cheered as Dale Earnhardt christened the new lighting system with the first practice lap.

All systems were in place for The Winston on May 16, 1992, billed as One Hot Night. It was an event that propelled NASCAR Winston Cup racing into prime-

On April 15, 1992, Bruton Smith flicked the switch to the elaborate lighting system at Charlotte Motor Speedway, and Dale Earnhardt was the first to cut a few quick practice laps under the glow of the artificial lights. A crowd of 38,000 was on hand for the historic evening. *CMS Archives*

Dale Earnhardt skids through the third turn in the final lap of the 1992 The Winston as Kyle Petty and Davey Allison slip past. Earnhardt was leading the event entering the final lap. The spin knocked him down to 14th in the final order. *CMS Archives*

time bonanza. The grandstands were packed with near-ly 140,000 spectators. What they witnessed was a charismatic splendor and a finish earmarked for NASCAR's historical archives.

Under the electric glare of the lights, the gladiators scampered gleefully lap after lap with a hungry pack in futile pursuit. The 70-lap format, broken down into two 30-lap segments and a 10-lap final dash, narrowed down to a battle between Dale Earnhardt, Kyle Petty, and Davey Allison. Earnhardt led entering the final lap. Down the back chute, Petty made his move to the inside but Earnhardt blocked the attempted pass. When the pair reached the third turn, Earnhardt's Chevrolet broke loose and spun. Petty lifted for an instant, which gave Allison momentum and an opening.

Allison and Petty crossed the finish line in a near dead heat with Allison inches ahead. The two cars banged together just after the finish line, sending Allison's Ford spinning into the concrete barrier.

The trackside audience was stunned. Rescue workers tended to the injured Allison, removed him from the demolished car, and took him to the infield medical infirmary. Team owner Robert Yates and crew chief Larry McReynolds spoke briefly with Allison before he was transported to the Carolinas Medical Center, suffering from a concussion, a bruised lung, and bruised legs. The battered Robert Yates Racing Ford was towed

Davey Allison plows into the wall along the front chute immediately after taking the checkered flag to win the 1992 The Winston. Allison and Kyle Petty crossed the finish line side by side and the two cars banged together. Allison was shaken up in the crash and was unable to participate in the Victory Lane ceremonies. *CMS photo by David Chobat*

Dale Earnhardt and crew chief Kirk Shelmerdine discuss race strategy prior to the 1992 Coca-Cola 600. Earnhardt didn't take the lead until the 347th lap, but once he grabbed first place he was not seriously challenged. It turned out to be Earnhardt's only triumph during the 1992 season. *CMS Archives*

to Victory Lane, where the ceremonies proceeded as scheduled without the winning driver.

Crowding the Winston Cup stars for the headlines during the 300- and 600-mile doubleheader weekend was youthful Jeff Gordon, whose reputation had been carved in the adventurous realms of open wheel racing. At age 20, Gordon was in his second full season in the NASCAR Busch Series and had already signed a long-term contract with Hendrick Motorsports for the 1993 Winston Cup season.

Gordon started on the pole for the Champion 300 and wowed the spectators with his imposing knowledge of strategy and crisp tactics. He took the lead with a daring move in tight traffic and ran away from the field, finishing well ahead of runner-up Bobby Labonte. The seeds

had been planted for a starburst career, and it underscored the certainty that Gordon's accomplishments would continue to flourish.

Dale Earnhardt, leading the final 54 laps, bagged his first win of the season in the 33rd annual Coca-Cola 600 on Sunday. Earnhardt started 13th, interrupted Ford's Winston Cup winning streak at 13, and ended a personal 13-race losing streak.

The chase for the 1992 NASCAR Winston Cup title took some jagged, unexpected twists late in the campaign. In mid-September, Bill Elliott seemed to have a lock on the championship, leading Davey Allison by 154 points and Alan Kulwicki by no fewer than 278 points. But three weeks later, when the teams began unloading their equipment for the Mello Yello

Jeff Gordon flashes under the checkered flag a single car length ahead of Michael Waltrip to win the 1992 All Pro Bumper-to-Bumper 300. Gordon, driving the Bill Davis–owned No. 1 Ford, swept both NASCAR Busch Series events in 1992. *CMS Archives*

escaped unscathed, and made it back to the finish line just ahead of Michael Waltrip. The race ended under the caution flag.

Mark Martin edged Kulwicki by 1.88 seconds to win Sunday's 500-miler as Elliott and Allison were mired in the mother lode of mediocrity the entire afternoon. Elliott eventually departed with a broken sway bar while Allison finished five laps down in 19th place. The point standings were a wide-open affair after the 500 with Elliott ahead by 39 points and Kulwicki only 47 points out of first place.

Kulwicki authored one of the most inspiring championship runs ever cataloged in the annals of NASCAR history by snatching the title in the last race of the 1992 season. A heavy underdog throughout the campaign, Kulwicki pulled an upset for the ages. Sadly, the self-styled loner had taken his last ride at Charlotte Motor Speedway. He perished in a plane crash in April of 1993.

The opening 10 races of the 1993 season were flavored with dominance from Rusty Wallace and Dale Earnhardt. The two dynamic warriors were running first and second in the point standings on the strength of having between them won half the races.

In the ninth annual The Winston, Earnhardt added a few more sparkling flakes of glitter to his dazzling portfolio of speed. On a double-file restart with two laps remaining, Earnhardt broke out of a side-by-side battle with Mark Martin, took the lead with a daring dive into the third turn, and scored his third win in the celebrated All-Star event. A sellout audience of 144,500 watched the show under starry skies.

Michael Waltrip prevailed in a hard-fought Champion Spark Plug 300 on Saturday, taking the lead from Ernie Irvan with eight laps remaining. "I'm tickled to death," said Waltrip in Victory Lane. "I love Charlotte Motor Speedway, and to finally win here on the home

500, Elliott's advantage had been narrowed to 67 points over Allison. Kulwicki was 144 points back.

Kulwicki put his affectionately nicknamed Ford "Underbird" on the pole for the Mello Yello 500 and applied a little midweek pressure on his rivals. Bill Elliott qualified 16th, while Allison logged the 22nd fastest time.

Saturday's All Pro Auto Parts 300 featured a second straight victory for Jeff Gordon at Charlotte Motor Speedway. A late caution flag for a four-car crash momentarily blocked the track in the fourth turn. Gordon narrowly avoided Robert Pressley's spinning car,

track of our [Bahari' Racing] team is even better than I dreamed it would be."

Sunday's Coca-Cola 600 got the green flag at 4:30 p.m., the first time the 600 began in daylight and ended under the glow of electric light. It was a tense twi-night affair subdivided by classic Earnhardt deliverance. Overcoming a series of penalties during the course of the race—one for alleged rough driving, one for speeding on pit road, and another for having too many crewmen over pit wall during a routine stop—Earnhardt shell-shocked the competition with a breathless comeback in the closing laps.

Earnhardt was a lap behind with 73 circuits remaining. But he was able to scramble atop the leader board just 35 laps later. He held a firm grip on first place and outran runner-up Jeff Gordon to nab his fifth triumph at Charlotte. "I'm really excited about winning the first 600 to finish under the lights," said Earnhardt. "It's history and it'll always be special."

The summer and early autumn of 1993 continued to be a personal playground for Earnhardt and Wallace. Together, they had won 14 of the 26 Winston Cup events with Charlotte's Mello Yello 500 next on the slate.

In Wednesday's qualifying, Jeff Gordon earned his first career pole for Sunday's 500-miler, tripping the timing clocks at 177.684 miles per hour. Ernie Irvan, who had taken the reins of the Robert Yates Racing Ford in the wake of Davey Allison's tragic demise in a helicopter crash, grabbed the other front row starting spot.

Saturday's All Pro Auto Parts 300 was won by Mark Martin, who overcame a penalty for pitting when pit road was closed and motored to a 1.14-second victory over Michael Waltrip.

The Mello Yello 500 was a record-setting event bathed in blinding speed and defused fireworks. Ernie Irvan jumped into the lead at the outset and kept his Texaco Havoline Ford up front the entire way. He led all but six laps when he was making routine, scheduled pit stops. Only two cautions interrupted his brisk pace, and his average speed for the 500 miles was a record 154.537 miles per hour. Mark Martin, Dale Earnhardt, Rusty Wallace, and Jeff Gordon rounded out the top five.

Earnhardt went on to win the 1993 NASCAR Winston Cup championship, his fifth title in the last eight years and his sixth overall.

Mark Martin leads a high-speed freight train into the first turn at the speedway during the 1993 All Pro Bumper-to-Bumper 300. Martin is the all-time race winner in NASCAR's Busch Series, and six of those victories have come at Charlotte. *CMS Archives*

Six weeks after the tragic death of Davey Allison, Ernie Irvan was selected to take over the controls of the Robert Yates Ford. In the 1993 Mello Yello 500, Irvan delivered a near-perfect effort, leading all but six laps en route to an overwhelming victory. *CMS Archives*

CHAPTER 14

New Stars Shine at Night

1994–1996

As the curtain began to rise on the 1994 season, the landscape in NASCAR Winston Cup racing was undergoing a dramatic change. A tragic fatal accident during practice at Daytona had plucked veteran Neil Bonnett from life's center stage. Harry Gant was preparing to kick off his farewell tour, and many struggling veteran drivers had been struck down by hit-and-run years, trying to get the license number of fleeting fame.

Waiting in the wings, however, was a youthful brigade of hard chargers yearning for experiences of the wildest, adventurous sort—hoping for an opportunity to showcase their developing talents. The roster included young lions Jeff Gordon, Bobby Labonte, Jeremy Mayfield, Joe Nemechek, John Andretti, and brothers Jeff and Ward Burton, all of whom had no more than a year's experience in Winston Cup. Each lived on raw natural ability, and all seemed destined to succeed in the often jagged world of big-time NASCAR racing.

Jeff Gordon paces the field in the early laps of the 1994 Coca-Cola 600. The promising sophomore took the lead with nine laps to go and scored his first NASCAR Winston Cup race in his 42nd career start. *CMS Archives*

John Andretti was the first driver to compete in the Indianapolis 500 and the Coca-Cola 600 on the same day. While his adventures at Indy were good enough to earn 10th place, Andretti had problems in the 600. His Billy Hagan Chevrolet was banged up in a couple of collisions and eventually fell out due to mechanical failure. *CMS Archives*

Dirk Stephens (No. 15) and Tim Bender (No. 36) skid to the apron after crashing in the 30th lap of the 1994 All Pro Bumper-to-Bumper 300 NASCAR Busch series event as Jimmy Hensley (No. 20) steers clear to the high side. The incident eliminated both Stephens and Bender while Hensley, filling in for an injured Randy LaJoie, continued and eventually finished ninth. *CMS Archives*

While the future generation sparkled on occasion, the veterans stood firm their ground. Sterling Marlin cracked Victory Circle for the first time in 278 starts in the 1994 season, opening Daytona 500. Dale Earnhardt, going for his record-tying seventh NASCAR Winston Cup championship, had won three times in the spring. Ernie Irvan, in the saddle of Robert Yates' powerful mount, had also won three races and held a narrow point lead when the tour came to Charlotte Motor Speedway for the annual May speed festivities.

John Andretti mapped out an ambitious schedule for Memorial Day weekend, attempting to become the first driver to compete in both the Indianapolis 500 and Charlotte's Coca-Cola 600 on the same day. With precious few minutes to spare, Andretti would take a jet from Indianapolis to the Charlotte area, hop a helicopter, and arrive trackside in time to saddle up for the 600. "I've been training like a marathoner," said Andretti. "God willing, it will be the ultimate race day."

The Charlotte Motor Speedway track record fell during qualifying for the Winston Open. Joe Nemechek buzzed around the track at a 181.519-miles-per-hour clip to establish a new speed standard and earn the pole for the 75-mile event. He was crowded by two other young guns, Ward and Jeff Burton, who qualified second and third. Jeff Gordon turned in the sixth-quickest time trial.

Gordon steered clear of an 11-car crash and won the Winston Open, leading the final 21 laps. Trailing Gordon at the wire were Greg Sacks, Ken Schrader, Jeff and Ward Burton, and Nemechek. The first six finishers advanced to the 10th annual The Winston Select.

Geoff Bodine recovered from an early spin and nabbed the 105-mile The Winston Select, a wild, crash-strewn affair that featured four lead changes in the final 10-lap dash. For Bodine, it was his first triumph since purchasing the team from the estate of Alan Kulwicki, the late 1992 NASCAR Winston Cup champion. "We dedicate this victory to Alan Kulwicki," said Bodine. "This is really special, even better than when we won the 1986 Daytona 500."

Before a crowd of 50,000, Jeff Gordon recorded his second career pole during Wednesday evening's first round of qualifying for the 35th annual Coca-Cola 600. Nemechek would flank him on the front row. Andretti qualified ninth-fastest, but would have to relinquish that spot for the 600 since there was no chance he could arrive from Indianapolis in time to attend the Sunday afternoon driver's meeting.

Phil Parsons ended an 11-year void by winning Saturday's Champion Spark Plug 300, his first triumph in the NASCAR Busch Series since winning at Bristol

in 1983. Parsons whipped his Chevrolet around Mark Martin with 18 laps remaining and sprinted to victory. Fate and recurring setbacks had prevented Parsons from experiencing seasons that were constantly rewarding, and he claimed the Charlotte win was more important than his lone Winston Cup victory at Talladega in 1988. "This is bigger than Talladega," he said. "My career was on the upswing then. Now I'm trying to get back across the fence into Winston Cup."

John Andretti finished 10th in the Indianapolis 500, his fourth consecutive top-10 finish at the Brickyard. In the next 2 hours, 27 minutes, Andretti used one golf cart, two police escorts, two helicopters, and one all-terrain vehicle to make the trip from Indianapolis to Charlotte Motor Speedway. At 4:49 p.m. Andretti stepped out of a helicopter in the infield and dashed to his car. The Coca-Cola 600 started at 5:13 p.m. Andretti made history for his Herculean effort, but his outing in the 600

was interrupted by a spin and terminal engine problems, which left him with a 36th-place finish.

Rusty Wallace hustled from his 21st starting spot to scramble into contention in the early going. He took the lead for the first time on the 164th lap and proceeded to pace the thundering herd most of the remaining distance. Wallace was leading when he made his final pit stop 26 laps from the finish. Staggered pit stops brought each of the front runners in for tires and fuel in the waning laps. Wallace, as did virtually all the other leaders, took on four tires for the final chase. Gordon made his final pit stop in the 381st lap, but crew chief Ray Evernham ordered a two-tire change only, and Gordon returned to the track ahead of Wallace. When temporary leader Ricky Rudd made his final stop with nine laps to go, Gordon breezed into the lead.

Gordon held his advantage over the final laps, finishing 3.91 seconds in front of Wallace. It was a

Bobby Labonte's Pontiac erupts into flames after slamming into the wall in the fifth lap of the 1994 Mello Yello 500. Sterling Marlin (No. 4), Joe Ruttman (No. 80), Bill Elliott (No. 11), Dale Earnhardt (No. 3), and Morgan Shepherd take quick evasive action. Labonte escaped from his burning car unharmed.
Bryan Hallman

Brothers Terry (No. 5) and Bobby Labonte (No. 18) battle for top honors in the 1995 Coca-Cola 600. Bobby prevailed in the tense struggle and earned his first trip to Victory Lane in a NASCAR Winston Cup event. It was the second year in a row the 600-mile produced a first-time series winner. *CMS Archives*

breakthrough triumph for Gordon. All of the promises of youth had been delivered in the stressful 600-mile sojourn. "This is the greatest day of my life," said a teary Gordon in Victory Lane. "That last lap I was just trying not to hit the wall because of all the tears coming down my face. This is a memory and a feeling that I'll never forget."

Ernie Irvan finished in fifth place and held a 62-point lead over Dale Earnhardt in the Winston Cup standings. Two months later, however, Irvan suffered debilitating injuries in a practice crash at Michigan International Speedway, which would remove him from racing's center stage for over a year. When the tour returned in October, Earnhardt enjoyed a comfortable 208-point lead and had a virtual lock on his seventh championship.

Irvan made his first public appearance in Charlotte Motor Speedway's garage area during the week of the Mello Yello 500. "It's a great feeling to see a lot of my friends and people who supported me. My goal in life right now is to be able to get back in the car and race again. It's my life," said Irvan.

Terry Labonte won Saturday's All Pro Bumper-to-Bumper 300 ahead of Mark Martin and Derrike Cope, an event in which Winston Cup drivers swept the first three places.

Ward Burton established a new track record in qualifying and won the pole for the 500 with a 185.749-mile-per-hour lap, a standard that has yet to be surpassed.

Sunday's 35th annual Mello Yello 500 featured a furious late race duel between Dale Jarrett, Morgan Shepherd, and Dale Earnhardt. Jarrett never led until grabbing first place with four laps remaining. Shepherd and Earnhardt followed closely. None of the top three

Bobby Labonte is greeted by Charlotte Motor Speedway chairman and chief executive officer Bruton Smith following his triumph in the 1995 Coca-Cola 600. Labonte led the final 43 laps after Ken Schrader's engine failure halted his victory bid. *CMS photo by Chuck Burton*

Jeff Gordon and mentor Ray Evernham take time out from the hectic schedule for a quiet moment in the garage area. The crew chief is a coach of sorts, digesting reams of information and forming a precise plan of attack. Evernham, Gordon, and the Hendrick Motorsports team combined for seven victories en route to the 1995 NASCAR Winston Cup championship. *CMS Archives*

finishers started in the top 20. For Jarrett, it was a sweet comeback. He had failed to qualify for the race at North Wilkesboro a week earlier.

Earnhardt breezed to his seventh NASCAR Winston Cup title, finishing 444 points ahead of runner-up Mark Martin.

Earnhardt was focused on winning his eighth championship as the 1995 season unfolded. With his Richard Childress team intact, he was the odds-on favorite to repeat once again as master of NASCAR's thunderbolt domain. Principal contenders figured to be Rusty Wallace and Mark Martin, and little preseason attention was given to Jeff Gordon and the Hendrick Motorsports team.

Earnhardt was atop the standings when the touring professionals came to Charlotte Motor Speedway for the annual May extravaganza. Following closely was Martin, who trailed by nine points, while Gordon, winner of three races, was only 15 points behind in third place.

In the 11th annual running of The Winston Select, Gordon dodged three crashes that sidelined eight cars and ran away from the field when the chips were down.

The NASCAR Sportsman division, born in 1989, featured retired Winston Cup automobiles and eager, hungry drivers yearning for superspeedway experience. From 1989 to 1995, the series made 42 stops at four different tracks. Thirty of the Sportsman events were presented at Charlotte Motor Speedway. Tim Bender was the top driver in the series, winning seven races. The Sportsman series, while providing plenty of excitement and close racing, was disbanded in 1995 following several nasty crashes. *Bryan Hallman*

Humpy Wheeler, president of Charlotte Motor Speedway, has one of the most active minds in motor racing. He is a jack of all trades and master of many, including a brief stint as a race car driver, a columnist for a racing trade paper, director of Firestone's involvement in NASCAR racing, and an auto racing promoter for nearly 40 years. His extravagant pre-race shows have become legend. *CMS photo by Chuck Burton*

Dale Earnhardt and Darrell Waltrip blasted past Gordon at the outset of the final 10-lap sprint, but they collided as they raced door-to-door in the fourth turn. "Dale got under me so I thought I'd go ahead and let them fight it out," said Gordon, who took the low groove when the leaders crashed. "We were three abreast going into turn three. I looked ahead and said there's no way they're going to make it through turn four. Sure enough, they didn't."

Firmly implanted in the favorite's role, Gordon won the pole for the 36th annual Coca-Cola 600 with an event-record 183.861-miles-per-hour clocking. Bobby Labonte, new driver for the Joe Gibbs Chevrolet team, earned the other front row starting spot.

Chad Little won Saturday's fog-shrouded Red Dog 300, his fourth victory of the 1995 season in the NASCAR Busch Series. Little pushed his Ford to the front with 18 laps remaining and held off Jeff Green in a spirited duel in the final laps.

Pole-sitter Gordon was in a prime position to take a giant stride in the point race with challengers Martin and Earnhardt shacked back in the field in 32nd and 34th starting spots, respectively. Gordon led 37 laps early in the race but fell from contention when a wheel broke in the 80th lap. He eventually finished 33rd.

Bobby Labonte became the second driver in as many years to record his first Winston Cup victory in the 600, outrunning brother Terry to the finish. It was the first one-two finish for brothers in NASCAR's premier series since Bobby and Donnie Allison did it in the 1971 World 600. "To win at Charlotte feels awful great," said the 31-year-old Labonte. "Charlotte is a tough place. It's a feeling I can't put into words right now. I don't think this has sunk in yet."

Earnhardt left Charlotte with an 80-point lead. Gordon had fallen to fourth, 101 markers behind, but he hit stride in the summer, building a 302-point lead over Earnhardt by October.

Ricky Rudd and Ricky Craven pulled mild upsets in qualifying for the UAW-GM 500 on pole night, while Gordon settled in the third starting slot. Earnhardt was forced to take a champion's provisional and started last in the 43-car field.

Mark Martin led five times for 167 laps and scampered to victory in the 23rd annual All Pro Bumper-to-Bumper 300 on Saturday. Dale Jarrett finished third with Busch Series regular Jeff Purvis third.

Martin then became the third driver to win both the 300 and 500 on the same weekend, matching the feat by Bobby Allison (1978) and Dale Earnhardt (1986). Following final green-flag pit stops, Martin trailed Terry Labonte by six seconds, but with fresh rubber on his

Pole-sitter Ricky Rudd (No.10) and outside front row starter Ricky Craven (No.41) lead the field to the green flag in the 1995 UAW/GM Quality 500. The new fourth turn grandstand was packed and the event set a record for attendance in an October event at Charlotte Motor Speedway. *CMS Archives*

Half the field in the 1996 International Race of Champions (IROC) race was involved in a grinding crash early in the 100-mile event. The cars of Dale Earnhardt, Steve Kinser, Robby Gordon, Al Unser, Jr., Terry Labonte, and Tommy Kendall were knocked out or severely damaged in the melee. Mark Martin was ahead of the crash and cruised to an easy victory.
CMS Archives

Roush Racing Ford, he was able to gradually erase the deficit. Martin slashed under Labonte with four laps remaining and motored to victory. Earnhardt squeezed past Labonte in the final lap to take second place. Gordon was slowed by rear gearing failure, which cost him 14 laps in the pits. He struggled to finish 30th and lost 97 points to Earnhardt in the point chase.

Earnhardt, madcap, rambunctious, and always spectacular, made a valiant charge in the final three races, but the 1995 season ended with Gordon clinging to a 34-point margin. At age 24, Gordon had become the youngest NASCAR Winston Cup champion since 23-year-old Bill Rexford won the title in 1950.

Through the first 10 events on the 1996 NASCAR schedule, Earnhardt was once again leading the Winston Cup standings in quest of his eighth national driving title. He held a 115-point cushion over Daytona 500 winner Dale Jarrett and was 131 and 187 points

in front of Hendrick Motorsports teammates Terry Labonte and Gordon.

Charlotte Motor Speedway was host to its most ambitious May schedule in history. The International Race of Champions (IROC) made its first appearance, and the Automobile Racing Club of America (ARCA) returned for the first time since 1964. The usual Winston Cup and Busch Series events made it a smorgasbord of speed for every racing enthusiast.

Mark Martin led the entire distance to win the 100-mile IROC race. An eight-car collision was triggered when Gordon and sprint car icon Steve Kinser rubbed fenders and spun. When the smoke cleared, only five cars were left undamaged. Tim Steele won a pair of double-header ARCA races that were staged five days apart.

Jimmy Spencer hustled to victory in the 75-mile Winston Open, earning a spot in the 12th annual

When Waltrip pulled into Victory Lane, his eyes were spinning like a slot machine in Las Vegas. "I ain't supposed to win this race," said a stunned but overjoyed Waltrip. "I'm shocked. I didn't really think I could win this thing. I figured Dale and Terry might overdo it. I laid back to have room to duck past them."

Mark Martin rallied from a lap deficit and won Saturday's Red Dog 300 in impressive fashion. Dick Trickle followed in second place as Winston Cup drivers took 11 of the top 12 spots.

Dale Jarrett had the field covered in the 37th annual Coca-Cola 600, leading 199 of the 400 laps, including all but eight of the final 174 laps. Jarrett powered his Robert Yates Ford to an 11.9-second triumph over Dale Earnhardt.

By October, Hendrick Motorsports stablemates Gordon and Terry Labonte were heading the point chase. Gordon, entering the UAW-GM Quality 500 on a three-race winning streak, was ahead by 111 points with four races remaining.

Mark Martin performed his usual flawless exercise in Saturday's All Pro Bumper-to-Bumper 300, leading the final 65 laps en route to his third straight Busch Series victory at Charlotte Motor Speedway. Bobby Labonte and Sterling Marlin gave futile chase in the closing laps.

Terry Labonte took a big bite out of Gordon's point lead on Sunday, winning the 500-mile classic. Taking the lead in a flurry of final-round green-flag pit stops, Labonte finished 3.84 seconds in front of Mark Martin to score his first Winston Cup victory at Charlotte Motor Speedway. Gordon had started on the front row and led in the early going, but was hampered by overheating problems and wound up 31st, 15 laps off the pace. He left Charlotte clinging to a one-point lead in the NASCAR Winston Cup standings.

Labonte, winner of two races during the season-long grind in 1996, took the NASCAR Winston Cup championship by 37 points over 10-time winner Jeff Gordon, capitalizing on the intricacies of the point structure, whereby consistency is more important than excellence during the annual chase for Winston Cup supremacy.

One of the most joyous Victory Lane celebrations came in the 1996 The Winston Select when Michael Waltrip produced the biggest upset in the history of the NASCAR All-Star contest. Waltrip, driving the Wood Brothers Ford, earned the final transfer spot from the preliminary Winston Open and came from the rear of the field to post his biggest career win. *CMS Archives*

The Winston Select All-Star field. Michael Waltrip finished fifth in the Open and took the last transfer spot in the 20-car The Winston field. Waltrip, winless in 309 official Winston Cup events, drove his Wood Brothers Ford into 10th place at the end of the opening 30-lap segment. He advanced to fourth in the middle portion and started fourth for the final 10-lap dash for cash.

With nine laps remaining, Dale Earnhardt slid up the track, crowding leader Terry Labonte. The upper groove duel left the bottom side wide open and Waltrip pounced on the opportunity. He shot into the lead and held his mount ahead of all pursuers the rest of the way.

CHAPTER 15

The Wonder Years

1997–1999

In four short years Jeff Gordon had become NASCAR's paramount subject. A NASCAR Winston Cup championship had been tucked safely in his portfolio in just his third full year on the tour, and a dynamic 10-race victory skein in 1996 was unapproached, although it only netted him second place in the fickle realm of the point standings.

All the physical promises of youth had been delivered. Although only 25 years old when the curtain lifted on the 1997 NASCAR Winston Cup season, Gordon had all the poise, composure, intelligence, and resilience of a seasoned veteran. With crew chief Ray Evernham serving as mentor, the team hit the ground with its wheels spinning swiftly.

Jeff Burton drove his Roush Racing Ford to a million-dollar victory in the 1999 Coca-Cola 600, beating Bobby Labonte in a close finish. Burton was one of the contestants in Winston's No Bull Five bonus program, having finished in the top five at Las Vegas in March. *CMS photo by Tom Riles*

Jeff Gordon drove a wildly painted Jurassic Park/DuPont Chevrolet in the 1997 The Winston and easily won his second NASCAR All-Star event. Equipped with a "new generation chassis" as crew chief Ray Evernham described it, Gordon came from the rear of the field, methodically worked his way into contention, and smoked his rivals in the final laps. *CMS photo by Terry Renna*

Joe Nemechek thunders into the high-banked turn ahead of Mark Martin and Dale Earnhardt, Jr. in the 1997 Carquest Auto Parts 300. The native Floridian was clearly the class of the field in the 300-lapper, leading for 134 of 200 laps. He nosed out Kevin LePage by 1.64 seconds to score his first victory at Charlotte Motor Speedway. *CMS Archives*

Gordon nabbed the Daytona 500 with an electrifying late-race charge. He won at Rockingham a week later, outrunning the dominant Dale Jarrett in another patented kick in the waning laps. Through the first 10 races of the 1997 campaign, Gordon had won four times.

Unveiling a new "future generation chassis," as Evernham described the car Gordon was set to drive in the 13th annual The Winston All-Star race, the Rainbow Warriors found themselves in the final row at the start. Gordon overshot his pit during the unique three-lap qualifying run, which included a pit stop. By not finishing his time trial, Gordon was forced to take the 19th starting spot. Ricky Craven had filled the 20-car field with his win in the Winston Open.

Stock car racing's "Wonder Boy" slashed through the field in the first 30-lap segment, finishing third. Following customary procedure, the field was inverted for the second 30-lap jaunt. Gordon started 16th, ran through the field again and slid home fourth. The final 10-lap dash found Gordon in the second row, and it took him only two laps to zip around his rivals and into the lead. Never seriously challenged once taking command, Gordon eased across the finish line comfortably ahead of runner-up Bobby Labonte to take the $207,500 first prize.

His stout run against heavy odds perplexed many of his beaten foes. "That car of his was really fast," said Mark Martin, who finished a distant sixth. "He could have won this race with one arm tied behind his back."

Seventh-place finisher Dale Jarrett said, "When it came time for Gordon to go, he went. I guess he did all he could do to make it look good. Nobody could touch him tonight."

Gordon's prototype car was held out of the 38th annual Coca-Cola 600, but he still captured his fourth straight pole position at Charlotte Motor Speedway for the 600.

Joe Nemechek prevailed in Saturday's Carquest 300 NASCAR Busch Series event, a heart-warming triumph for the native Floridian who lost his brother John in a crash two months earlier in a NASCAR Truck series event. "He was with me there," said a choked-up Nemechek in Victory Lane. "John was right there with me. He was my brother, my best friend, everything."

Weather perilously threatened the Coca-Cola 600, scheduled for a 6:15 p.m. green flag. An afternoon thunderstorm delayed the start by 26 minutes. Gordon led 17 laps in the early going, but the handle went away on his Hendrick Motorsports Chevrolet and he drifted out of immediate contention. Bobby Labonte, Dale Jarrett, Bill Elliott, Jeff Burton, and Ernie Irvan took turns pacing the field.

At 8:40 p.m., seven laps short of halfway, rain brought out the caution flag. NASCAR officials, with the interests of the 140,000 spectators at heart, put down the red flag two laps later—just before the race

Joe Nemechek is bussed by wife, Andrea, and mother, Martha, in Victory Lane following a spirited drive in the 1997 Carquest 300. Nemechek led the final 69 laps and scored his first win since his younger brother John lost his life in a NASCAR Truck Series event two months earlier at Homestead, Florida. *CMS photo by Chuck Burton*

would have become an official event. It wasn't until 11:35 p.m. that the race resumed.

At 12:18 a.m. early Monday morning, NASCAR officials informed the teams that the checkered flag would be waved after 333 laps had been completed, 100 miles short of the scheduled distance. When the decision was made, 20 laps remained before the 333-lap mark.

Rusty Wallace was leading but Gordon was on the prowl and closing ground rapidly. Gordon shot past Wallace 17 laps from the finish and sprinted to his fifth win of the season. Seemingly out of the hunt most of the way, Gordon galloped past all challengers when the money was on the line.

Veteran motorsports reporter Mike Mulhern said Gordon's late race kick "left his rivals back in the garage simply stunned. Gordon was incomparable, a veritable Houdini, all but shackled and blindfolded yet still able to wiggle free and escape to victory."

By October, Gordon had scored five more victories and had climbed into the favorite's role in the championship chase. He came to Charlotte Motor Speedway with a 135-point lead over Mark Martin in the Winston Cup standings.

The Silver Anniversary running of Saturday's All Pro Bumper to Bumper 300 NASCAR Busch Series race was won by Jimmy Spencer, who staved off a late challenge by Mark Martin to prevail in a thrilling contest. "This is special," said Mr. Excitement after scoring his first Charlotte win. "This is Charlotte. I've wanted to win one of those funny-looking trophies for a long time, and now I finally have one."

Sunday's 38th annual UAW-GM Quality 500 was won by Dale Jarrett, who led the final 57 laps and outran runner-up Bobby Labonte by 4.1 seconds. Dale Earnhardt wound up third, with title contenders Martin and Gordon following in fourth and fifth, respectively.

Gordon held on to win his second Winston Cup championship trophy by a scant 14 points over Dale Jarrett, who put on a furious rally at the end of the year. Mark Martin wound up third in the standings, only 29 points behind. It was the closest three-way championship race in NASCAR Winston Cup history.

The 1998 campaign was earmarked as the Golden Anniversary of NASCAR, a marketing blitz that was one of the most ambitious in the history of America's most successful motorsports sanctioning body.

The 50th Anniversary began on a warm Cinderella note as Dale Earnhardt prevailed in the Daytona 500, a magical prize that had eluded his grasp for 19 years. The coverage by the mainstream media was electric.

Robby Gordon (No. 14) and Ernie Irvan crashed heavily in the 209th lap in the 1996 UAW-GM Quality 500. Irvan's Ford broke loose in the second turn and was nailed by Gordon's Chevrolet. Both drivers were knocked woozy in the incident. *CMS Archives*

Jeff Gordon prevailed in a soggy, rain-abbreviated Coca-Cola 600 in 1997, passing Rusty Wallace for the lead with 17 laps remaining. The victory placed Gordon in a position to win the Winston Million, a $1 million bonus for winning three of the series' five annual crown jewel events. He bagged the prize at Darlington in September, becoming the first man to win the bonus since 1985. *CMS photo by Chuck Burton*

Five different drivers prevailed in the first five races of the 1998 NASCAR Winston Cup season. By late May, Jeremy Mayfield was atop the point standings with two-time winner Jeff Gordon ranked third and Mark Martin, winner of three events, hanging onto fifth place.

Gordon started fourth on the grid in the 14th running of The Winston All-Star event and sailed into the lead by the fourth lap. He ran away with the first 30-lap segment, easily beating Bobby Labonte and Mark Martin.

The top four positions were inverted for the second 30-lap chase. Martin, starting second, led the entire distance as Gordon ran second. During the second intermission, all drivers made pit stops, but the crew's efficiency and strategy entered into the equation. For the first time in the history of the event, the order the cars came off pit road determined the order for the restart. In years past, all cars lined up in the order in which they had finished the second segment.

Gordon pitted for two tires on the pit stop and returned to the track in the lead. The Rainbow Warriors decided against adding any fuel during the quick stop. Martin took on four tires and lined up fifth for the final restart. After an aborted start, which took two additional laps, the field flashed under the green flag. Gordon took off and left his rivals scrambling for second place.

Flashy Tony Stewart, who captured three open wheel titles in a single season, competed in the 1997 All Pro Bumper-to-Bumper 300 at Charlotte in October 1997. Carving a new career on four wheels, and most effectively so, Stewart finished an impressive third behind Jimmy Spencer and Mark Martin. *CMS photo by Harold Hinson*

As Gordon took the white flag, his car slowed with an empty fuel tank.

Martin, who had passed Bobby Labonte for second moments before Gordon abruptly slowed, cruised into the lead and held Labonte at bay in the final lap. "He slowed down as he got the white flag," said Martin. "I thought he was just going to let me catch up and make a show of it. But he never got going again. It's a tough break for those guys."

Gordon coasted to a 12th-place finish and was clearly despondent afterward. "I would rather run in the middle of the pack or at the tail of the field instead of taking the white flag and run out of gas and lose like this," he said.

Martin dashed past a sputtering Jimmy Spencer with five laps remaining to win Saturday's Carquest 300, his fifth NASCAR Busch Series win at Charlotte Motor Speedway.

Pit strategy by Evernham and a brilliant come-from-behind charge by Gordon in the Coca-Cola 600 made amends for the gaffe during The Winston. Running a distant fifth, the resilient young warrior received a gift-wrapped opportunity when Gary Bradberry spun on lap 378, bringing out the final caution of the evening. The leaders all pitted for two fresh tires, but Evernham opted for four new tires on Gordon's mount.

The final restart came with 16 laps remaining, with Gordon running sixth. Gordon quickly hustled his way past Johnny Benson, Dale Jarrett, and Mark Martin, then set his sights on Rusty Wallace and Bobby Labonte, both of whom were going for a million-dollar bonus for winning the 600. After Gordon, Wallace, and Labonte rode for some time in dramatic three-abreast formation, Gordon ducked under Wallace and Labonte in one fell swoop on lap 391 and grabbed the lead. He was never challenged the rest of the way and laid claim to his third Coca-Cola 600 triumph in the last five years.

"All of the ups and downs we have had this week, I think it brought us closer together and made us more motivated and more focused for this race," said Gordon, who also took the point lead for the first time in the 1998 season. By late summer, Gordon had surged to a healthy point lead, winning seven of nine Winston Cup events over one stretch. The team stumbled briefly on pole night, qualifying a disappointing 26th.

In Saturday's 26th annual All Pro Bumper-to-Bumper 300, Mike McLaughlin ran the final 93 laps (139.5 miles) on one tankful of fuel and coasted home a half-lap ahead of Matt Kenseth to score his first Charlotte victory.

Mark Martin prevailed in Sunday's wreck-strewn 500-miler, an event that had 11 caution flags, including

Dale Jarrett scored his third NASCAR Winston Cup win at Charlotte in the 1997 UAW-GM Quality 500. An accidental chassis adjustment allowed Jarrett to scamper away from all challengers in the closing laps. A rubber spacer spring fell from the left front of his Robert Yates Ford and Jarrett said the car developed better handling characteristics. *CMS photo by Harold Hinson*

As the teams and spectators gathered for the annual pilgrimage to Daytona to kick off the 1999 season, an important announcement took place on Speedway grounds on Tuesday, February 9. Chairman of the board and chief executive officer Bruton Smith announced that Lowe's Home Improvement Warehouse, Inc., had signed a blockbuster 10-year, $35 million deal whereby, effective immediately, the plush facility was to become known as Lowe's Motor Speedway.

"Lowe's has been connected with motorsports for a number of years," said Smith. "With Lowe's being a long-standing, very reliable North Carolina-based company, it makes this announcement very special. We have been impressed with their growth and sports marketing efforts."

Lowe's Motor Speedway president H. A. "Humpy" Wheeler said, "The new trend in sports marketing has been selling the naming rights at various venues. I think it is significant for us to be the first in the motorsports industry to do this. We continue to find ways to be innovative in motorsports marketing and facility management."

Bob Tillman, chief executive officer of Lowe's Home Improvement Warehouse, Inc., added, "This makes perfect sense for us because we both have the same target market. Of all sports-marketing activities, this one yields the highest return of all because the fan loyalty is greater in NASCAR than [in] any other sport."

9 for crashes. The rugged Arkansas native was virtually home free after Bobby Labonte spun in the 203rd lap, triggering a wreck that involved nine of the cars that were running in the top 15.

Gordon finished in fifth place in the 500, enabling him to keep a solid grip on the point lead. He also went on to win three of the last five races on the 1998 calendar, running his victory total to 13, the most wins in a single season since Richard Petty won 13 in 1975. His final margin of victory in the championship was 364 points over Martin.

In May 1999, freshman sensation Tony Stewart was attempting to become only the second driver to compete in the Indianapolis 500 and the Coca-Cola 600 on the same day. The days leading up to the daily double were as stressful and physically demanding as the big race day. On Saturday, May 22, Stewart qualified for the Indianapolis 500, received a police escort to a nearby airport and 2 hours and 4 minutes later was

Third-generation driver Dale Earnhardt, Jr., pits his Chevrolet during the 1998 Carquest 300. The 1998 NASCAR Busch Series campaign was Earnhardt, Jr.'s, first full season, but the lineage of one of America's fastest families continued as he won the championship on the strength of seven race wins. *CMS photo by Harold Hinson*

Special paint schemes are a staple of the modern NASCAR racing scene. Dale Jarrett's Batman-flavored Ford, paired up with Terry Labonte's conventionally painted Kellogg's Chevrolet, had a strong run in the 1998 Coca-Cola 600, finishing in fifth place. *CMS photo by Harold Hinson*

Tony Stewart hoists the winner's trophy high above his head after winning the 1999 Winston Open. Pulling triple duty by qualifying for the Indianapolis 500, Stewart won the Open and ran second in The Winston All-Star event. He came back the following week and finished ninth in the Indy 500 and fourth in the Coca-Cola 600. Stewart's iron man achievements remain among the Herculean efforts in motorsports. *CMS photo by Harold Hinson*

Dale Earnhardt, Jr., made his NASCAR Winston Cup debut in the 1999 Coca-Cola 600 at the newly named Lowe's Motor Speedway. The 24-year-old youngster qualified 8th on the grid and drove a smooth and intelligent race in the 600, coming home 16th. *CMS photo by Tom Riles*

on the track in Charlotte at Lowe's Motor Speedway, practicing for the Winston Open.

Stewart won a 25-lap qualifier to gain a front-row starting position for the Open, then won the 50-lapper in dominating style to gain admission to the 15th annual All-Star race. He nearly pulled that one off as well, leading until six laps from the finish when Terry Labonte sped into the lead for good. Stewart finished a close second.

Sharing the incredible hype with Stewart during the 40th anniversary running of the Coca-Cola 600 was Dale Earnhardt, Jr., who was preparing to make his NASCAR Winston Cup debut. The 24-year-old third-generation driver qualified eighth for the 600 while Stewart timed 27th fastest.

Earnhardt, Jr., was one of 15 drivers competing in both the Carquest 300 and the Coca-Cola 600. He finished a close second to Mark Martin. Jeff Gordon competed in his first NASCAR Bush Series race at Lowe's Motor Speedway since 1992, placing 33rd after mechanical problems sent him to the garage near the halfway point.

Stewart finished ninth in the Indianapolis 500 after starting 24th, completing 490 of the 500 miles. At 5:44 p.m. in Charlotte, Stewart landed in a helicopter near the front stretch of Lowe's Motor Speedway. Having missed the driver's meeting, he had to start from 43rd. Stewart whipped his Pontiac through the field and led three times for 14 laps. He was in contention for the win until late in the race, when he faded while on the edge of exhaustion.

Stewart collapsed when the race was over. "I felt I let our guys down a little bit in the last 25 laps," he reflected later. "I started feeling fatigued, hadn't eaten well, and that's what caused me to feel ill late in the race."

Jeff Burton squeezed past Bobby Labonte with 17 laps remaining and sped to his first victory at Charlotte's Lowe's Motor Speedway, earning a million-dollar bonus as one of R.J. Reynolds No Bull Five contenders. Labonte, also going for the million, settled for second. Mark Martin was third and Stewart fourth. Earnhardt, Jr., finished 16th in his big-league debut.

Jeff Gordon, paired with new crew chief Brian Whitesell, scored his second-straight NASCAR Winston Cup victory in the record-setting 500-miler. Only two brief cautions interrupted the event; Gordon averaged 160.306 miles per hour. Point leader Dale Jarrett finished seventh to protect his cushion in the championship chase. At the conclusion of the 1999 NASCAR Winston Cup season, Jarrett was accorded the sport's highest honor, becoming only the second driver in history to win the championship his father had won before him.

The October speedfest featured a dramatic last-lap victory for Michael Waltrip in the All Pro Bumper-to-Bumper 300 on Saturday.

Heavy rains on Sunday forced postponement of the UAW-GM Quality 500 until Monday morning, the first complete rainout at Lowe's Motor Speedway since 1968.

In its 40 years of existence, Charlotte's Lowe's Motor Speedway has advanced from a ramshackle structure to a vision of architectural excellence. With astute leadership, the facility has provided an inestimable value to the growth of NASCAR stock car racing and has become the nucleus for a skyrocketing sport as the new millennium begins.

Mark Martin and Matt Kenseth dual their Roush Racing Fords during the 1999 UAW/GM Quality 500. Martin finished fourth in the rain delayed contest and Kenseth gave a good account of himself until an accident sidelined him midway through the event. *Bryan Hallman*

Mike Skinner (No. 31) and Jeff Gordon (No. 24) engaged in a spirited battle for top honors in the 1999 UAW-GM Quality 500. Skinner led for 62 laps and nearly pulled off his first Winston Cup Victory, but had to settle for third at the finish. Gordon led only for a total of 16 laps. He took the lead for the final time with only eight laps remaining. *Bryan Hallman*

Charlotte Motor Speedway 600-Mile Race Results

Year	Race Winner	Car	Speed	Pole Winner	Car	Speed
1960	Joe Lee Johnson	Chev	107.735	Fireball Roberts	Pont	133.904
1961	David Pearson	Pont	111.633	Richard Petty	Plym	131.611
1962	Nelson Stacy	Ford	125.552	Fireball Roberts	Pont	140.150
1963	Fred Lorenzen	Ford	132.417	Junior Johnson	Chev	141.148
1964	Jim Paschal	Plym	125.772	Jimmy Pardue	Plym	144.346
1965	Fred Lorenzen	Ford	121.722	Fred Lorenzen	Ford	145.268
1966	Marvin Panch	Plym	135.042	Richard Petty	Plym	148.637
1967	Jim Paschal	Plym	135.832	Cale Yarborough	Ford	154.385
1968	Buddy Baker	Dodg	104.207	Donnie Allison	Ford	159.223
1969	LeeRoy Yarbrough	Merc	134.361	Donnie Allison	Ford	159.296
1970	Donnie Allison	Ford	129.680	Bobby Isaac	Dodg	159.277
1971	Bobby Allison	Merc	140.422	Charlie Glotzbach	Chev	157.788
1972	Buddy Baker	Dodg	142.255	Bobby Allison	Chev	158.162
1973	Buddy Baker	Dodg	134.890	Buddy Baker	Dodg	158.051
1974	David Pearson	Merc	135.720	David Pearson	Merc	157.498
1975	Richard Petty	Dodg	145.327	David Pearson	Merc	159.353
1976	David Pearson	Merc	137.352	David Pearson	Merc	159.132
1977	Richard Petty	Dodg	137.676	David Pearson	Merc	161.435
1978	Darrell Waltrip	Chev	138.355	David Pearson	Merc	160.551
1979	Darrell Waltrip	Chev	138.674	Neil Bonnett	Merc	160.125
1980	Benny Parsons	Chev	119.265	Cale Yarborough	Chev	165.194
1981	Bobby Allison	Buic	129.326	Neil Bonnett	Ford	158.115
1982	Neil Bonnett	Ford	130.058	David Pearson	Buic	162.511
1983	Neil Bonnett	Chev	140.707	Buddy Baker	Ford	162.841
1984	Bobby Allison	Buic	129.233	Harry Gant	Chev	162.496
1985	Darrell Waltrip	Chev	141.807	Bill Elliott	Ford	164.703
1986	Dale Earnhardt	Chev	140.406	Geoff Bodine	Chev	164.511
1987	Kyle Petty	Ford	131.483	Bill Elliott	Ford	170.901
1988	Darrell Waltrip	Chev	124.460	Davey Allison	Ford	173.594
1989	Darrell Waltrip	Chev	144.077	Alan Kulwicki	Ford	173.021
1990	Rusty Wallace	Pont	137.650	Ken Schrader	Chev	173.963
1991	Davey Allison	Ford	138.951	Mark Martin	Ford	174.820
1992	Dale Earnhardt	Chev	132.980	Bill Elliott	Ford	175.479
1993	Dale Earnhardt	Chev	145.504	Ken Schrader	Chev	177.352
1994	Jeff Gordon	Chev	139.445	Jeff Gordon	Chev	181.439
1995	Bobby Labonte	Chev	151.952	Jeff Gordon	Chev	183.861
1996	Dale Jarrett	Ford	147.581	Jeff Gordon	Chev	183.773
1997	Jeff Gordon	Chev	136.745	Jeff Gordon	Chev	184.300
1998	Jeff Gordon	Chev	136.424	Jeff Gordon	Chev	179.647
1999	Jeff Burton	Ford	151.367	Bobby Labonte	Pont	185.230

Charlotte Motor Speedway 400- and 500-Mile Results

Year	Race Winner	Car	Speed	Pole Winner	Car	Speed
1960	Speedy Thompson	Ford	112.905	Fireball Roberts	Pont	133.465
1961	Joe Weatherly	Pont	119.950	David Pearson	Pont	138.577
1962	Junior Johnson	Pont	132.085	Fireball Roberts	Pont	140.287
1963	Junior Johnson	Chev	132.105	Fred Lorenzen	Ford	143.017
1964	Fred Lorenzen	Ford	134.475	Richard Petty	Plym	150.711
1965	Fred Lorenzen	Ford	119.117	Fred Lorenzen	Ford	147.773
1966	LeeRoy Yarbrough	Dodg	130.576	Fred Lorenzen	Ford	150.533
1967	Buddy Baker	Dodg	130.317	Cale Yarborough	Ford	154.872
1968	Charlie Glotzbach	Dodg	135.234	Charlie Glotzbach	Dodg	156.060
1969	Donnie Allison	Ford	131.271	Cale Yarborough	Merc	162.162
1970	LeeRoy Yarbrough	Ford	123.246	Charlie Glotzbach	Dodg	157.273
1971	Bobby Allison	Merc	126.140	Charlie Glotzbach	Chev	157.085
1972	Bobby Allison	Chev	133.234	David Pearson	Merc	158.539
1973	Cale Yarborough	Chev	145.240	David Pearson	Merc	158.315
1974	David Pearson	Merc	119.912	David Pearson	Merc	158.749
1975	Richard Petty	Dodg	132.209	David Pearson	Merc	161.701
1976	Donnie Allison	Chev	141.226	David Pearson	Merc	161.223
1977	Benny Parsons	Chev	142.780	David Pearson	Merc	160.892
1978	Bobby Allison	Ford	141.826	David Pearson	Merc	161.355
1979	Cale Yarborough	Chev	134.266	Neil Bonnett	Merc	164.304
1980	Dale Earnhardt	Chev	135.243	Buddy Baker	Buic	165.634
1981	Darrell Waltrip	Buic	117.483	Darrell Waltrip	Buic	162.744
1982	Harry Gant	Buic	137.208	Harry Gant	Buic	164.694
1983	Richard Petty	Pont	139.998	Tim Richmond	Pont	163.073
1984	Bill Elliott	Ford	148.861	Benny Parsons	Chev	165.579
1985	Cale Yarborough	Ford	136.761	Harry Gant	Chev	166.139
1986	Dale Earnhardt	Chev	132.403	Tim Richmond	Chev	167.078
1987	Bill Elliott	Ford	128.433	Bobby Allison	Buic	171.636
1988	Rusty Wallace	Pont	130.677	Alan Kulwicki	Ford	175.896
1989	Ken Schrader	Chev	149.863	Bill Elliott	Ford	174.081
1990	Davey Allison	Ford	137.428	Brett Bodine	Buic	174.385
1991	Geoff Bodine	Ford	138.984	Mark Martin	Ford	176.499
1992	Mark Martin	Ford	153.537	Alan Kulwicki	Ford	179.027
1993	Ernie Irvan	Ford	154.537	Jeff Gordon	Chev	177.684
1994	Dale Jarrett	Chev	145.922	Ward Burton	Chev	185.759
1995	Mark Martin	Ford	145.358	Ricky Rudd	Ford	180.578
1996	Terry Labonte	Chev	143.143	Bobby Labonte	Chev	184.068
1997	Dale Jarrett	Ford	144.323	Geoff Bodine	Ford	184.256
1998	Mark Martin	Ford	123.188	Derrike Cope	Pont	181.690
1999	Jeff Gordon	Chev	160.306	Bobby Labonte	Pont	185.682

Charlotte Motor Speedway May Late Model Sportsman and Busch Series Results

Year	Race Winner	Car	Speed	Pole Winner	Car	Speed
1961	Bill DeCoster	Ford	128.116	n/a	n/a	n/a
1965	Ralph Earnhardt	Ford	123.906	Sonny Hutchins	Ford	142.030
1978	Morgan Shepherd	Pont	116.409	Bob Pressley	Chev	157.311
1979	Darrell Waltrip	Chev	131.243	John Anderson	Chev	162.984
1980	David Pearson	Pont	118.773	David Pearson	Pont	165.874
1981	Morgan Shepherd	Pont	115.212	Dave Marcis	Pont	162.234
1982	Harry Gant	Pont	126.731	Harry Gant	Pont	162.847
1983	Dale Earnhardt	Pont	117.724	Morgan Shepherd	Olds	161.565
1984	Bobby Allison	Olds	126.198	L.D. Ottinger	Pont	162.421
1985	Tim Richmond	Pont	119.284	Tim Richmond	Pont	160.633
1986	Tim Richmond	Pont	139.715	Tim Richmond	Pont	163.711
1987	Harry Gant	Buic	139.643	Brett Bodine	Olds	167.328
1988	Dale Jarrett	Olds	139.969	Geoff Bodine	Chev	168.099
1989	Rob Moroso	Olds	136.450	Greg Sacks	Pont	167.214
1990	Dale Jarrett	Pont	132.337	Dick Trickle	Pont	168.219
1991	Dale Earnhardt	Chev	133.235	Jack Sprague	Olds	167.167
1992	Jeff Gordon	Ford	127.208	Jeff Gordon	Ford	170.638
1993	Michael Waltrip	Pont	127.539	Tracy Leslie	Chev	172.574
1994	Phil Parsons	Chev	127.704	Mike Skinner	Chev	172.480
1995	Chad Little	Ford	131.707	Rich Bickle	Ford	173.193
1996	Mark Martin	Ford	155.799	Dale Jarrett	Ford	171.996
1997	Joe Nemechek	Chev	126.954	Mark Martin	Ford	175.012
1998	Mark Martin	Ford	133.449	Bobby Labonte	Pont	172.822
1999	Mark Martin	Ford	119.377	David Green	Chev	176.569

Charlotte Motor Speedway October Late Model Sportsman and Busch Series Results

Year	Race Winner	Car	Speed	Pole Winner	Car	Speed
1961	Wally Dallenbach	Ford	n/a	n/a	n/a	n/a
1973	Bobby Allison	Chev	139.788	Bobby Allison	Chev	155.409
1974	Bobby Allison	Chev	119.973	Bobby Allison	Chev	154.250
1975	Ray Hendrick	Chev	118.214	L.D. Ottinger	Chev	158.311
1976	Ray Hendrick	Chev	116.845	L.D. Ottinger	Chev	159.466
1977	Darrell Waltrip	Chev	135.904	Darrell Waltrip	Chev	160.409
1978	Bobby Allison	Mata	131.068	Darrell Waltrip	Chev	160.810
1979	Darrell Waltrip	Pont	118.033	Darrell Waltrip	Pont	163.058
1980	Dave Marcis	Pont	119.960	Dave Marcis	Pont	163.340
1981	Gary Balough	Pont	135.678	Jody Ridley	Pont	164.539
1982	Darrell Waltrip	Pont	123.458	Phil Parsons	Pont	162.191
1983	Sam Ard	Olds	141.269	Larry Pearson	Pont	162.235
1984	Darrell Waltrip	Pont	123.499	Tim Richmond	Pont	163.676
1985	Terry Labonte	Pont	140.485	Geoff Bodine	Pont	162.656
1986	Dale Earnhardt	Chev	138.746	Dale Earnhardt	Chev	161.599
1987	Harry Gant	Buic	131.868	Harry Gant	Buic	168.940
1988	Rob Moroso	Olds	123.683	Harry Gant	Buic	169.710
1989	Rob Moroso	Olds	126.035	Michael Waltrip	Pont	168.993
1990	Sterling Marlin	Olds	132.272	No Time Trials	NTT	NTT
1991	Harry Gant	Buic	121.937	Ward Burton	Buic	172.574
1992	Jeff Gordon	Ford	120.954	Jeff Gordon	Ford	173.566
1993	Mark Martin	Ford	113.960	Bobby Dotter	Chev	174.390
1994	Tery Labonte	Chev	134.831	Mark Martin	Ford	176.696
1995	Mark Martin	Ford	136.415	Bobby Dotter	Chev	172.051
1996	Mark Martin	Ford	124.957	Bobby Labonte	Chev	174.272
1997	Jimmy Spencer	Chev	127.089	Joe Nemechek	Chev	176.378
1998	Mike McLaughlin	Chev	145.376	Dave Blaney	Pont	177.247
1999	Michael Waltrip	Chev	133.325	Matt Kenseth	Chev	177.328